BABY'S
~ FIRST YEAR ~

BABY'S
~ *FIRST YEAR* ~

Ros Meek

WARD LOCK LIMITED · LONDON

© Ward Lock 1989
© Illustrations Ward Lock 1989

First published in Great Britain in 1989
by Ward Lock Limited, 8 Clifford Street
London W1X 1RB, an Egmont Company

Line illustrations by John Woodcock

Text filmset in Monophoto Sabon
by MS Filmsetting Limited, Frome, Somerset

Printed and bound in Great Britain by
William Collins, Glasgow
British Library Cataloguing in Publication Data

Meek, Ros
Baby's first year
1. Babies. Home care, – Manuals – For parents
I. Title   II. Series
649'.122

ISBN 0-7063-6778-2

I would like to take this opportunity to thank my parents,
especially my mother, for the many sacrifices that they made in
order to provide a happy childhood for me, to say nothing of all
the help and support that they have given me in bringing up my
own children.

CONTENTS

INTRODUCTION

There are many reasons why you may have decided to buy this book. Perhaps it's your first baby and you are feeling uncertain about how it will grow and develop. Maybe your baby is older and you want to know how long it will be before you have a settled night, or perhaps you need some advice about weaning. Whatever the reason, I hope that you will be able to find the help or reassurance that you need.

All babies are different. It doesn't matter if this is your first or your fourth, each baby is an individual and will have different likes and dislikes. The challenge is to find out what makes your baby happy and contented.

If your baby was born before forty weeks of pregnancy or weighed less than 2.3 kg (5 lb) then its needs will be different from those of a full-term baby of 3.2 kg (7 lb). The feeding pattern will be more frequent with the baby taking smaller amounts than a larger baby, even though the babies may have been born on the same day. Premature babies will develop normally, but it may take them a few extra months to sit or stand.

Included in this book is a guide to the month-by-month development of a 3.2 kg (7 lb) baby. Remember to allow extra time if your baby was born before thirty-six weeks of pregnancy. The guidelines are only a rough idea of what your baby may be able to do. Sometimes you may find your baby is more ahead in one area of development than would be expected at that age. If you feel that your baby is not developing along the lines suggested in the chart, ask your health visitor or GP. They will be pleased to help you and ready to listen to any concerns however small.

Having a baby is an easy time to make friends. Neighbours and passers-by are all interested in the new arrival. The clinic is also a good place to meet others with babies of a similar age. There is a lot of support that can be gained if you meet up together regularly. The babies can get to know each other and the mothers can learn from the likes and dislikes of other babies. Often your problem will shrink away as your hear about someone else's! Swopping and sharing information can be very helpful, but don't forget that all babies are different and that what works for one six-month-old baby may not be right for yours.

Make the most of your time with your baby, each phase passes so quickly. Many parents like to keep a photographic and written record of their baby's development: first words, funny and infuriating moments together. It's fun to look back.

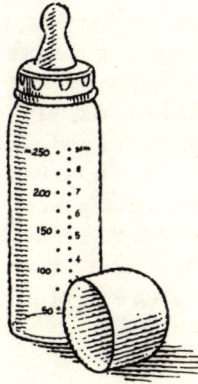

AFTER THE BIRTH

Some women prefer to blot out the whole experience of labour. This may be due to the fact that a partner was unable to be present, feelings of failure because the labour ended in a caesarean birth, or perhaps because it was more difficult or painful than had been imagined. Whatever the reason it is best to try to talk about the experience; most women have difficult moments during pregnancy and delivery, and the more these are bottled up the worse they may become. Talk to your midwife or health visitor. Ask her to explain anything that is bothering you. It may help just to talk, on the other hand you may have grounds for a complaint to the hospital. Either way talking will help. (For further information about how to complain, see page 12.)

Even if you have everything to be happy about, you may not be feeling back to normal yet. What is back to normal anyway? Many women, looking back over the first year of motherhood, say that it takes six-to-nine months to be physically and mentally fit again. After all it takes nine months of pregnancy to make a baby, so for some women it may take nine months to fully recover. What is important is that you tell someone how you are feeling so that help can be given. The health of the new mother is vital to the well-being of the baby, so tell your partner, mother, friend or health visitor. A problem shared is a problem halved.

PAIN

You may experience abdominal pains, similar to contractions, after childbirth. These are called after pains and often occur in the first weeks after delivery. They are sometimes triggered off by the hormone which is released when you start to breast-feed and are more common in second- and third-time mothers. They should only last a week or so, but if they cause severe discomfort speak to your GP or midwife. A couple of paracetamol tablets may help. On the positive side, it means that your uterus (womb) is returning to its pre-pregnancy size.

Pain from stitches or an episiotomy (incision made to help with second stage of labour) can be very severe. Don't be fobbed off. If your episiotomy hurts get someone to look at it. Some women find it a good idea to look for themselves – it seldom looks as bad as it feels! Pain in this area can be caused by infection, so make sure you have a soothing bath every day. Dry yourself well. If the pain persists or if the area looks more swollen and red than before, consult your doctor or midwife; it could be caused by a badly-placed stitch which can be eased. In a few cases it may be caused by poor stitching. If this is the case then make sure you get help (see page 41). Sitting on a rubber ring can ease the pain. Your local National Childbirth Trust (NCT) branch may be able to let you have one on loan (see page 107). Some women find that a pack of frozen peas placed on the stitches is helpful! It usually takes about a week-to-ten days to become more comfortable. If the episiotomy is still painful after this time, make an appointment to see your GP (see Postnatal check-up, page 41).

CONSTIPATION

If you suffer from constipation following the birth of your baby, try eating extra fresh fruit and vegetables, and make sure that you are drinking sufficient, especially if you are breast-feeding. A tablespoon or two of bran sprinkled on your breakfast cereal will also help. If you are still unable to open your bowels after three days ask your local pharmacist for a laxative. Do not get into the habit of relying on laxatives though, it is important that you get back to your normal routine.

BREASTS

If you are breast-feeding, your breasts will probably feel tender until your milk supply is established. Don't be tempted to drink less. If the tenderness becomes really uncomfortable ask your midwife to show you how to express just enough milk to ease the discomfort.

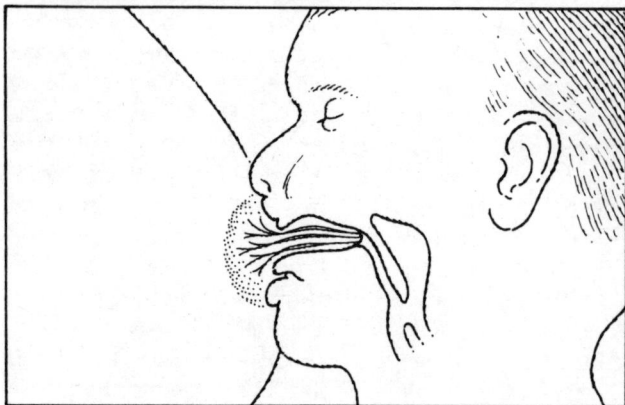

Sore or cracked nipples can be a problem, and they are usually caused by the baby's sucking position. Make sure that when the baby starts to feed, the mouth is wide open with the lower lip turned back touching the breast. Soreness is usually caused by the baby sucking on the tip of the nipple rather than taking most of the areola (ring of pigmentation surrounding the nipple) into the mouth. Cuddle your baby close to you so that it is easy for the baby to suck.

Nipple shields are sometimes suggested but there can be problems weaning the baby off them. They can also inhibit the milk supply as the baby does not stimulate the breast in the same way.

Thrush (a fungal infection) can also make your nipples sore. This will be seen in your baby's mouth as little white spots which, unlike milk curds, will not wipe off. If you suspect that the soreness is caused by thrush get some treatment for both of you from your doctor. It is important that you are both treated at the same time so that the infection is not passed back again.

If you are having problems getting breast-feeding established, ask for help from your midwife, health visitor or from a breast-feeding counsellor (see page 28).

TIREDNESS

No matter how good the baby is, most new mums suffer from lack of sleep. The fact that you are now responsible for another human being means that you are always aware of his or her needs and put these before your own. Try to make time for a rest during the afternoon when the baby is asleep. Leave the vacuuming, it can wait. Accept offers of help to take the baby for a walk or to allow you to nip down to the shops alone or have your hair cut. Encourage your partner to help care for the baby. If you can afford to buy disposable baby goods for a while use them and don't feel guilty. When you've had an exhausting day, don't forget the local take-away. If your tiredness seems to be getting too much for you, talk to your health visitor or GP.

YOUR WEIGHT

Most women take some time to get back to their pre-pregnancy weight and shape. Remember to do your postnatal exercises (see page 12). Don't be tempted to diet. Right now, you need to be eating well to breast-feed and to have the stamina to cope. Look at what you are eating and when. If you feel ravenous before your partner returns home, adjust your meal time and have a cup of tea with him later. If you feel that you have a serious weight problem talk it over with your GP or health visitor – they may run a slimming class or know of one which you can join.

HOW TO COMPLAIN
1. Try to write down what you feel went wrong and why. Do this as soon as possible.
2. If you complained whilst in hospital, who was it to and what did they say or do?
3. Were there any witnesses? (Your partner? Midwife?)
4. Contact AIMS (Association for the Improvement of Maternity Services, see page 105) for further advice. If AIMS feels that you have a case which should be answered it will give you advice about how to go about it.
5. Remember to keep copies of any letters that you write. Your GP health visitor and local community health council may also be of help.
6. Tell them about the good things as well, so that they see you have a balanced judgement.

POSTNATAL EXERCISES

The daily regular exercises that are taught in the hospital by the obstetric physiotherapists are very important. At the time it's the last thing you feel you want to do, but the exercises can really help you to regain your figure and help your 'insides' get back into shape, too.

The most important muscles to get working are the pelvic floor – these are the support-and-control muscles of the pelvis. Even if you have had stitches it is a good idea to start these exercises straight away. It is vital to make them strong again as they control your bladder function and also contribute to sexual satisfaction.

THE PART THAT FATHER PLAYS

The part that father plays in bringing up children has changed considerably over the past thirty years. These days a father is encouraged to help plan the pregnancy with his partner and to make sure that he, too, is as healthy as possible for the conception of their baby. Throughout pregnancy the father is actively encouraged to attend antenatal classes to help him to understand the changes that are happening to his partner. One of the biggest developments, though, has been the involvement of the father during labour.

Having attended antenatal classes, many fathers look forward to being with their partner during the actual labour. They take a keen interest in the progress of the baby's delivery, and the new technology that is used to make labour safer for both the mother and baby. Others may be extremely supportive to their partner, helping her with breathing, relaxation techniques, supporting her in different delivery positions and mopping her forehead from time to time.

To be present at the actual birth of the baby can be the culmination of many months of excited expectation tinged with anxiety for the father. The relief, coupled with the joy of seeing the baby for the first time, is always obvious on the father's face. For many it's a time of mixed emotions with a sense of wonder on the one hand and sense of responsibility on the other.

Some men prefer not to be present at the actual birth and this must be respected. Sometimes this can lead to a feeling of being let down for the woman, so it is helpful if the decision can be talked about before the actual birth. Many men are unsure about whether they want to be present, but, when the time comes, wild horses wouldn't drag them away.

The period immediately after birth is an emotional time for most women. Not only are they feeling exhausted from the birth, but visitors can be very tiring too. The following are jobs for fathers which may help:

Job 1
Keep visitors at bay! Of course, close relatives will want to come and see the baby, but that shouldn't mean half the pub and all the workmates, too!

Job 2
If you are able to take some time off work, now is the time to do it. It's a very precious time sharing and getting to know your baby.

Job 3
Help your partner to think about herself as well as the baby. Breast-feeding, in particular, is easier to get going when the partner is supportive. Any feeding is time-consuming, so be prepared to feel a bit left out.

Job 4
If you feel your partner is becoming depressed or has any physical symptoms, such as sore stitches or painful breasts, that don't seem to be getting better, talk it over with her. It can be difficult, particularly where depression is concerned, to help a partner to realize that she needs help.

Job 5
If the baby cries a lot or takes a long time to settle, offer to take him or her for a walk to the park while your partner has some time for herself.

Some dads don't find new babies very interesting. There seems to be little that they can do, and, even when they do offer, it's sometimes refused. If you feel a bit awkward or clumsy with the baby you will only get better if you persevere! Most babies respond well to men's firm handling. Tiny vests and nappies can all be mastered given time!

By taking part in the day-to-day care of your baby, you will be more aware of, and get more enjoyment out of, the rapid developmental changes that your baby goes through during the first year. As the baby reaches six weeks the first smiles are a breakthrough and character begins to form. There is no more welcoming a sight than an excited baby greeting you as you come through the door in the evening.

Day-to-day care will also enable you to experience some of the difficulties of caring for a baby. There will be some days when your home looks chaotic with piles of washing left around, kitchen in a mess and no meal ready. Be understanding – your usually efficient partner may have had a really trying day with the baby. It's amazing how the day can fly by when you are constantly feeding, cuddling and rocking a baby!

It will also help if your partner is able to voice the frustration she feels at times. This may occasionally spill over in anger and resentment at her loss of identity. After all, pregnancy and motherhood have been a major upheaval of her life. If either of you ever feel the sort of pressure that makes you feel you want to harm your baby, please seek help. Talk to your health visitor, GP or phone the local helpline (see addresses at back of book). It can help just to talk about your feelings, and the mood may pass. Severe financial hardship, redundancy and emotional upsets can all contribute to feelings of anger towards the baby.

Don't feel that you will be condemned if you ask for help, and don't fear that your child will be taken away from you unless you feel that it should. It's only extreme cases that ever get that far.

RELATIONSHIPS

Having a baby naturally involves certain changes in your life-style – the joy and wonder of a new person to love, the inability to have a full night's sleep, the extra washing and feeding, all take time to become accustomed to as part of a new routine.

Antenatal classes will certainly help you to think about the needs of your baby, and if your partner is able to go with you to the classes it will benefit you both. It's very hard for most men to understand the emotional changes that women go through after having a baby. Having a wife or girl-friend who dissolves into tears over something seemingly trivial can be bewildering. Antenatal classes will help the father understand that these moments are normal and that the more help he can give the better it will be.

Thoughts and feelings

On the one hand you will feel elated at having had your baby, on the other you may feel daunted by the challenge. You may feel that you do not really love your baby. You may feel tired or sore, or have problems with getting breast-feeding established. There are many different thoughts and feelings passing through and not enough time in the day for you and the baby, never mind your partner!

Don't let things get on top of you. If you feel you need more help, ask for it. Accept any offers to do a bit of cooking or shopping. Your partner will be able to help with things around the home. Involve him in everything – it will bring you closer together as you care for your baby. Remember, men can feel very left out in the early weeks. Your partner needs to feel involved with the nitty-gritty of baby care. Of course he can change nappies and bath the baby and if he is a bit awkward or clumsy it doesn't matter. Babies like firm handling and respond well to what may seem to you a bit rough.

'She's never got time for me.'

It is easy for a woman to become totally preoccupied with the baby in the first few weeks. It's a natural part of what is known as the bonding process, the way in which a mother and baby grow to love each other. If your partner is preoccupied, try to show her that you understand and care by cooking a meal and cleaning up afterwards; or suggest that she has a rest while you take the baby to the park or down to the shops. By giving her a break she will be able to relax a little and enjoy seeing you play your part. Try to arrange to get out together – ask one of the grandparents to babysit for an hour or two while you go down to the pub, or the cinema, or for a Chinese!

If things seem to be getting difficult try to talk about it. Sometimes the GP or health visitor can be helpful in these situations.

One part of a couple's relationship that may need a period of adjustment following childbirth is the sexual relationship. Some couples find that the baby brings them closer together, but others experience a distancing which can seem hard to resolve. Try to find time in the evening to sit together and have a cuddle. This doesn't have to lead to sex, but it can be very relaxing, enjoyable and healing to feel cared for in this way.

If, as a woman, you feel worn out, depressed or upset by the sight of your post-pregnancy body, then it's important to talk about why you don't feel ready for sex. It doesn't mean that your feelings have changed towards your partner, it's just that you need time to feel sexy again. Of course, the minute you do feel ready, the baby will wake up, but that's life!

There can be physical reasons why you are not feeling

ready to resume an active sex life. Stitches that have not healed well or an episiotomy (cut) that has been badly repaired. Speak to your doctor or health visitor if you suspect that this is causing the problem.

Men can also find it hard to resume a sexual relationship. Perhaps it's because they have been present through labour and delivery or perhaps they can't come to terms with your new role as mother as well as lover. Patience and understanding on both sides are needed (see also Postnatal Check List page 41).

'What about grandparents and older relatives?'

Relationships between in-laws can be tricky. Encourage help and sharing the care of your baby, but remember if you don't want your baby to be in a smoky atmosphere ask them to refrain from smoking while the baby is present. Listen to advice, but make up your own mind what you act on.

One of the biggest problems when you have a baby is conflicting advice given by all sorts of well-meaning people. Remember that you know your baby best, so do what you feel is right. Your health visitor will always be happy to discuss ideas that you might want to try.

'James seems a different child now we've got Donna, I just can't understand it.'

Older brothers and sisters need time to adjust to a new baby. Encourage them to help, and make sure that you give them your undivided attention at least once a day. Sharing a book together, or bathtime are good moments when the baby can be left in the pram or cot. If the child seems genuinely aggressive towards the baby, make sure they are not left alone together. Ask your partner to help out so that you and your first-born can go to the park or library together like old times. Gradually, the resentment will lessen but if you are worried speak to your GP or health visitor.

THE PRIMARY HEALTH CARE TEAM

When you have just had a new baby it can be very bewildering if people call offering you advice or wanting to look at your baby or yourself and expecting you to talk freely about the most intimate things. Often these so-called professionals assume you know who they are and what they do. You may never have met them before, so don't be afraid to ask who they are and ask them to explain why they are visiting you and for what purpose. You are responsible for your baby and anyone wanting to look at your child should have your consent. The only time when professionals are able to overrule a parent's wishes is if they have reason to believe the child is at risk of physical or emotional abuse.

When you come out of hospital a community midwife will come and visit you in your house. She will be interested in your baby and yourself. She will advise on breast- and bottle-feeding and general care of the baby. In some areas midwives visit you until the baby is fourteen days old, but in others they may visit until twenty-eight days.

HEALTH VISITORS

Health visitors are nurses who have had extra training in the health and development of babies and children up to five years. Your health visitor will help you and your family stay healthy both emotionally and physically and she will help you to work out what is best for you all. The health visitor is not visiting you to tell you what to do or check up on you, she will respect and value your ideas. Of course, if you do have any queries about yourself or your family's health she will be pleased to help you.

Your health visitor will be able to direct you to help

with the benefits and social security payments that you might be entitled to. As she works in your neighbourhood she will know what facilities and help are available, and she will be able to discuss childcare if you want to return to work. During your baby's first year, she will invite you to the child health clinic where you can go as often as you wish. There will always be a health visitor at the clinic, though it may not always be your own. This may be an advantage if you don't get on with yours!

The clinic is a very busy place and there may not be time for you to ask all the questions that you want to. You may not wish to discuss personal problems in this environment, so ask your health visitor to come and see you at home. Home visits are a very important part of the health visitor's job. Many mothers and fathers feel more relaxed in their own home, particularly if they want to discuss personal matters. Health visitors aren't just there for baby's well being, they are interested in all members of the family, young and old.

GENERAL PRACTITIONER

You will need to register your baby with your GP so that you are both on his or her list. Many GPs like to visit mothers and new babies in their home soon after birth. The GP may also run a baby clinic at which your health visitor may be present. A GP, whom you have got tó know during your pregnancy and who is friendly and supportive, can be very helpful during the postnatal period.

OBSTETRIC PHYSIOTHERAPISTS

These are specialist physiotherapists who can give you advice on keeping your body fit during and after pregnancy and birth. They can help with backache problems, sciatica and other aches and pains. In some hospitals the obstetric physiotherapists run postnatal exercise classes.

THE CHILD HEALTH CLINIC

Your health visitor will invite you to come to the clinic where she and a doctor will be on hand to give reassurance and advice. It's up to you how often you go, but most mothers find it helpful to go every two weeks. Your baby will be weighed and its weight and head measurement entered on a percentile chart. This chart monitors the baby's weight gain. Ask your health visitor to explain it to you.

The baby can have the developmental check-ups at the clinic together with immunizations (see page 22). You will be given a record book to keep so that you can see how your baby is putting on weight. The book will also have space to write in any illnesses that your baby may have and the date of injections. This information will be needed when your child starts school.

If the clinic doctor is also your GP, she can prescribe medicines for you and your baby. In some cases though the doctor will come from the local hospital and will, therefore, refer you to your doctor for treatment. Your views on your baby's health are important and you will probably be the first person to notice if there is a developmental or physical problem. Don't keep your worries to yourself, share them with a health visitor or doctor.

WORRIED ABOUT YOUR BABY?

All of us worry about our babies at one time or another, but worries can get out of proportion. If you feel there is something wrong, talk to your partner. He may have noticed it too. If after you've had a chat you still feel concerned, then have a talk with your health visitor or GP. They will treat your anxieties with sympathy and will regard you as the expert on your child. If you don't get the help you want ask someone else in the practice or in the clinic. After all, you know your baby best. (There are also many useful addresses at the back of this book.)

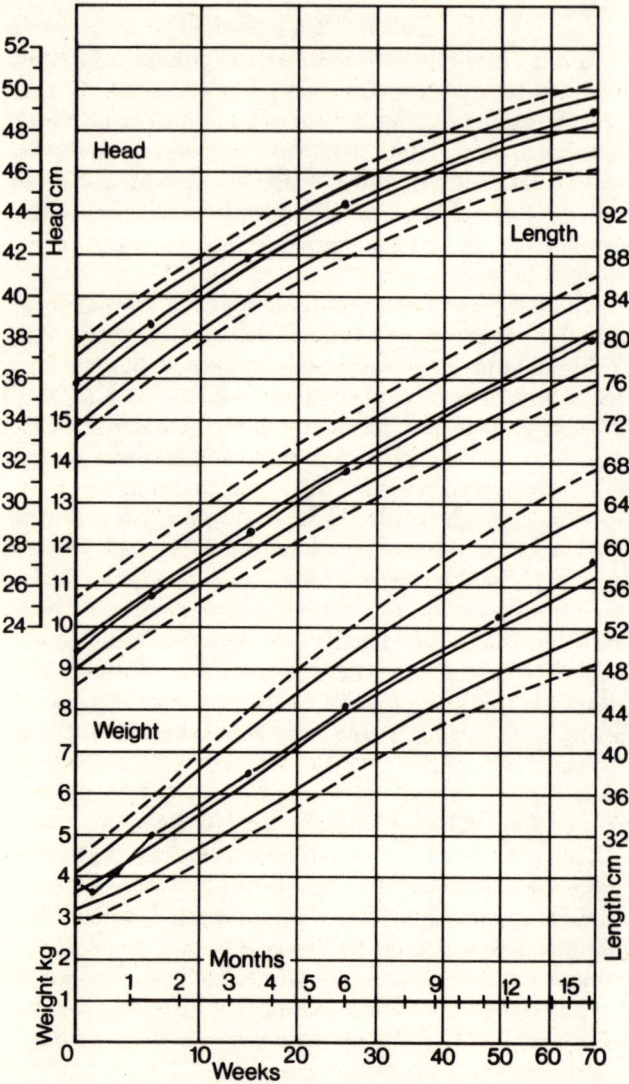

A boy's percentile chart, with a typical boy's growth pattern as plotted by a GP.

HANDICAPPED BABIES

One of the first emotions that parents feel when they are told that their baby is handicapped is overwhelming guilt. Mothers think back over the pregnancy and blame themselves for a party or night out which they feel may have harmed their baby. Guilt is a very common reaction, though it's very unlikely that anything the mother did during pregnancy is to blame.

Guilt changes to anger and sadness as parents grieve for the baby they had hoped for. What is most needed at this time is information from doctors, health visitors and parents of similarly handicapped babies. Your health visitor can be a vital lifeline for you at this time, liaising between hospital, GP and home, and asking questions that you may not feel able to ask. If you feel you need a friendly support during this stressful time ask your health visitor to accompany you to the hospital. She will understand your conflicting feelings and your worries for the future.

Almost all handicapped babies are diagnosed at birth or soon afterwards. This is why the regular developmental checks are so vital. There are a few handicaps that show up later and this can be a great worry to parents who feel that they have to keep convincing medical people that there's something wrong. Obviously it's not an easy thing to have to do or admit to, but it's best to speak about any worries you have so that your baby can be assessed accurately. The sooner your baby is diagnosed and helped the better it will be for all of you.

Contact-A-Family is a group which puts parents with physically or mentally handicapped children in touch with each other either individually or as local self-help groups. It can be reached at 16 Strutton Ground, London SW1P 2HP (Tel. 01-222 2695).

BABY'S FIRST MONTH

One of the first things that new mums do when they are left alone with their new baby for the first time, is have a good look at them. The feeling of amazement that this real live baby has come from you and your partner is incredible.

Before the baby leaves hospital he or she will be seen by a paediatrician who is a doctor specially trained in the care of babies and children. Take this opportunity to ask any questions that may have occurred to you during your stay. Paediatricians are used to the kinds of worries that new mothers and fathers have,

---

POSITION OF BABY'S BODY AND MOVEMENT

- Baby lies on its back with its head turned to one side. The arm on the same side is usually stretched out, or both arms are bent. Legs are bent up with knees apart.
- When the baby moves the arms are more active than the legs.
- If the cheek is touched the baby will turn its head to that side.
- If the ear is touched the baby will turn away.
- If you lift the baby into a sitting position the head will lag behind, and fall forwards when it reaches a sitting position.
- When baby lies on its tummy, the head will turn to one side and the arms and legs will be flexed under the body with bottom in the air, in a crawling position.
- If you stand the baby on a hard surface supporting it under the arms, it will press down on its feet and may make stepping movements.

so don't be shy. It's better to have questions answered than to retain them as worries.

When you look at your new baby you may wonder what is normal for a baby of this age. The milestones of development shown opposite are intended to help you.

What can baby see?
New babies stare blankly at walls or at a bright window. They are very short-sighted at birth. When examined by the doctor, the baby will shut its eyes tightly when the torch is shone into its eyes. It will also follow a rattle a short distance if this is held less than 15 cm (6 in) away.

By six weeks the baby will start to watch its mother's face when feeding.

What can baby hear?
New babies are startled by loud noises and may cry. When the doctor rings a bell close to its ear, movement will stop for a few seconds while baby listens.

If the baby is grizzling, a gentle voice will usually stop it for a short time.

What can baby do?
A new baby sleeps most of the time except when it's being fed, changed or handled.

New babies suck vigorously.

By about six weeks the baby will smile at familiar faces.

When the baby is picked up it will usually stop crying.

The baby has a strong grip in the first weeks of life. This weakens as it grows older.

CLOTHING
Babies need to be kept warm and draught free, but there is a danger of overheating. Remember to unwrap your baby when you come in from a shopping trip even when the baby is fast asleep.

BABY'S LAYETTE
Pram with safety straps
Cot and mattress
Baby bath
Nappy bucket with lid
Baby chair with safety straps ideally
   convertible to high chair
2 towels
24 nappies
4 cot blankets
4 cot sheets
4 sleeping suits
Shawl
4 vests
4 plastic sheets
3 pram sheets
3 pram blankets
2 matinée jackets
Bonnet
2 pairs mittens
2 pairs bootees
3 bibs
If bottle-feeding
6 feeding bottles and teats
Sterilizing unit

FEEDING – THE FIRST MONTH

By the time you come to read this book you will have already decided how you are going to feed your baby. Even though your decision has been made – it is helpful to look at the advantages and disadvantages of breast- and bottle-feeding.

Most health professionals agree that breast-feeding gives a baby the best start in life. But it's a sad fact that some women who are keen to breast-feed don't succeed. This can be for a variety of reasons, but usually it is because there has not been enough help and encouragement available. If you feel that breast-feeding is not going well, you need to get help. Your midwife, health visitor or breast-feeding counsellor (see page 35) can help you. Most of the problems can be overcome by very simple changes. Sometimes what seems to be a unique problem or a worry is something that happens to most women.

Most babies are put to the breast as soon as they are born. This is so that they can help the breasts to start work as soon as possible. Breast-feeding in these early days also helps your uterus to return to its normal size. The antibodies that are present in the first fluid the breasts make (colostrum) will protect your baby against many infections for up to two years. It is also thought

---

BREAST-FEEDING

Advantages

1. Milk always ready at correct temperature.
2. Milk changes to suit your baby's needs.
3. Breast milk contains antibodies which protect your baby against infection.
4. Breast milk can help prevent conditions such as asthma, eczema and food intolerance.
5. Breast-feeding is a source of comfort for the baby and satisfaction for you.
6. Breast-feeding is cheaper than bottle-feeding.

Disadvantages

1. Breast-feeding is sometimes difficult to get established, but with the right help, you should be able to succeed if you want to.
2. Until you are able to express breast milk in sufficient quantity, you will be the only person who can feed the baby.

that breast-feeding protects children from many child-hood cancers. Even if you only breast-feed for a few weeks you will be giving your baby a good start, but if you can manage it for longer the satisfaction that you will experience will be tremendous. If you have to stop breast-feeding for any reason, don't feel guilty. You may feel disappointed but you can still be a good mother and have a good relationship with your baby.

BREAST-FEEDING HELP STARTS HERE!

If you don't get into a good position you will get backache, neckache, aching arms and perhaps sore nipples, so ask your partner to help you get comfortable.

Positions to feed the baby:
Experiment with extra cushions or pillows to support your back and arms in order to raise the baby to the breast. Take the phone off the hook, have some tissues and a drink handy, and a book if you feel like it.

a) Sitting in a chair
Place a pillow on your lap to raise baby up so that you don't have to lean forward. Place a pillow under your feeding arm.

b) Rugby position
Place the baby on one or two pillows tucked under your feeding arm.

c) Lying down
This is particularly useful if you have had a caesarean section or a sore perineum – the tissues between the anus and the external genitalia – after childbirth. Lie down on your side with a pillow between your legs and a pillow under your head.

Supporting the breast

In the early stages of breast-feeding, the breasts feel hard and heavy as you start to feed. Wearing a good, well-fitted bra, designed for feeding, will help. Check that it doesn't rub or cause any pressure. Breast pads are essential, too, during the early weeks, to mop up excess milk. These pads are very absorbant and help to keep your clothes dry. You can either use disposable pads or buy washable ones. It is helpful to wear a bra during the night, too, in order to provide support.

Starting to feed

First of all make sure you are comfortable in whichever position you find most relaxing. Turn your baby in towards you so that you are 'chest to chest'. By placing your hand flat against your ribcage, lift your breast to enable the baby to latch on more easily. Allow your nipple to brush the baby's mouth and you will find the mouth will open. Make sure that the nipple and most of the areola is inside the mouth, and that the lower lip is turned back with the chin touching the breast. In this position the nipple is drawn right inside the baby's mouth and the aerola is gripped by the gums. Sore nipples are most often caused by a poor sucking position, so it is worthwhile spending some time making sure the baby is well 'latched on'. If the baby only sucks on the nipple the breast does not receive adequate stimulation and so, along with soreness, the milk supply may be affected.

If you find that feeding is painful ask your midwife or health visitor to watch you. An extra pillow or two may help the position or the baby may need to be encouraged to opens its mouth wider, so that it will no longer nipple-feed but breast-feed. If your nipples get so painful that you dread the next feed, then try hand-expressing your milk and give it in a bottle to your baby (ask your

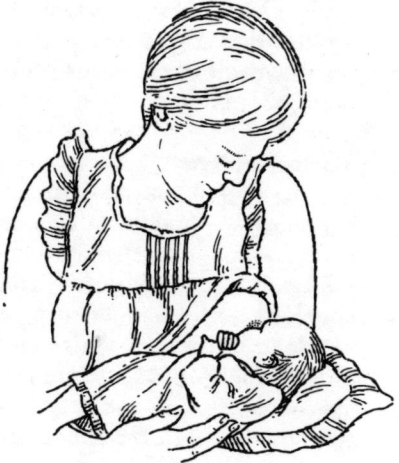

midwife or health visitor to show you). Although hand pumps are useful for expressing milk later on, they may be too rough on a sore breast. Nipple shields can help, but prolonged use of these can reduce the milk supply and may eventually cause the baby to reject the nipple in favour of the teat-like shield.

Thrush (a fungal infection) can also cause sore nipples. It is important that, if you suspect you have thrush, your baby is treated as well.

How often should baby be fed?

When the baby cries in the first few days it is usually because he or she is hungry. By feeding as often as the baby wants, the milk supply will be increased. Milk is made by demand and supply, so that the more the baby sucks, the more milk will be produced. Naturally if you feed more often you will make more milk.

When you start to breast-feed, your breasts will need a lot of stimulation to establish a good supply. Most babies feed more than seven times a day in the early stages. If your baby feeds less than this it may cause your supply to slacken off, but it may be that your baby has such a strong suck that enough is taken to maintain a good amount. If you don't think you are making enough milk the answer is to put the baby to the breast more frequently and allow him to finish the first side before offering the other. It may seem a chore to feed nine or ten times a day during the first week or so, but once you have established a good supply you should have few problems.

Opposite: Different breast-feeding positions. Choose whichever is most comfortable for yourself and baby.

How long should baby suck?

There are lots of different ideas about how long to let a baby suck. It's best to let the baby suck for as long as it wants to on one side before you change to the other. This is because there are two types of milk that are produced during a breast-feed – the fore milk and the hind milk. It's important that the baby gets enough of the hind milk as it is this that is most satisfying. Offer the baby the other breast, but don't be worried if the same amount of sucking does not take place. Remember, though, to start the next feed on this side. If you can't remember which side you started with, put a safety pin in your bra to remind you. If your baby wants to suck for a long time, then relax and let it suck for as long as it needs so long as you don't get sore. Don't time the feeds, the baby knows how much it needs and so long as you are prepared to feed as and when it seems to need one then it will be getting enough.

Is baby getting enough milk?

You will be encouraged to take your baby to the clinic to be weighed, but if your baby is generally content and has plenty of wet nappies (at least six each day) then you can rest assured that you are making enough milk. If you are worried then by all means attend the clinic regularly for reassurance, but remember that the way to increase the milk supply is by extra feeding and by looking after yourself.

Most babies establish their own feeding pattern by about six weeks, but, even so, they will have 'off' days when they seem to want feeding all the time. Don't see this as a failure on your part, just feed as often as the baby needs and the pattern will re-establish itself.

If you are told that your baby is under weight then offer the breast more frequently. You can also try waking your baby – some very sleepy babies lack the energy to wake up and cry for a feed.

Reasons for sore breasts

If your breasts appear lumpy and over full, then it is possible that you may have a blocked milk duct. Usually as the baby feeds any lumps disappear, but lumps that remain can become tender and inflamed. Often there seems to be no reason why they occur, but there are several things worth checking if you continually find you have lumps in your breasts:

- Make sure your bra fits well and is not too tight.
- When you feed, make sure you don't press the breasts continually, perhaps in an attempt to help the baby breathe more freely. The pressure can cause blockages.
- Avoid poor positioning which allows the baby to drag the nipple downwards.
- Avoid a poor sleeping position that causes pressure on the breasts by squeezing your breast between your body and arm.

How to help painful inflamed lumps

Many women find that hot or cold flannels placed on the breasts relieve pain and help to disperse the lumps. Very gentle downward massage towards the nipple will also help. After you have fed the baby it may help to express a little more milk. If the lumps seem to be near the armpit, swinging the arms or cleaning windows may help. These lumps and bumps rarely occur once breast-feeding is established, so persevere and talk to other breast-feeding mothers – they can provide the best reassurance.

Mastitis

If the skin around the lump becomes red and inflamed it may be that the breast has become infected. When this happens milk leaks out into the tissue around the milk ducts and causes a local soreness and infection. If you are feeling tired with flu-type symptoms, check that none of the pressures described above may have caused the problem. If you continue to feel uncomfortable, consult your GP. The doctor may prescribe antibiotics which will soon clear it up. If it is not treated a breast abscess may develop. There is no need to stop feeding even if you are taking antibiotics. The milk will not be affected by the inflammation or infection. Breast milk contains vital antibodies which will protect the baby from the infection and by the time you realize there is something wrong your baby will already have been feeding and in contact with the germs.

Don't give up feeding your baby at this time because the resulting build-up of unused milk will cause even more pressure on your sore breasts. Remember your baby is in no danger, but you may be caused a lot more pain and discomfort if you stop breast-feeding. Remember to tell your GP you are breast-feeding if he prescribes any drugs for you.

If the baby doesn't seem satisfied...

Because you can't see how much milk your baby is taking, doubts may sometimes creep in about whether you are making enough. If you have a bad day when all the baby seems to want to do is feed and be cuddled, don't worry, this is sometimes nature's own way of increasing the milk supply. Don't be put off, just feed the baby more often, even waking the baby if you feel the gap between feeds is too long. Some mothers find the baby needs more feeds when three to six weeks old – a growth spurt.

You can also try:
- Having your baby in bed with you for the night feeds, so that you can doze.
- Taking the opportunity to put your feet up when your baby sleeps so that you have

enough energy for the rest of the day.
- Remembering to have sufficient to eat and drink. It doesn't have to be fancy food, a good sandwich made of wholemeal bread with cheese and salad filling, and a cup of tea or coffee, will help you through the day. If you're hungry you will be on edge and less able to cope. Your health is just as important as your baby's.
- Avoiding complementary feeds of baby milk, water or juice. Remember the only way to increase the milk supply is by letting the baby suck on your breasts. Teats will confuse the baby and may lead to rejection later. It's fine to express breast-milk and feed it in a bottle occasionally, but be careful about doing it too often in the early stages. When milk is expressed, partners are able to feed the baby and give you a break.

Do you feel like giving up?

While your baby is asleep think about why you want to give up. Maybe you are having a bad day and tomorrow will be better. Perhaps you have eaten something which may have disagreed with the baby. Some foods which *can sometimes* cause babies discomfort are peas, chilli or very spicy food, garlic, red wine, grapes, oranges and strawberries. This doesn't mean you have to avoid them, just introduce them with caution.

Speak to your health visitor or midwife who will have had lots of experience where breast-feeding is concerned. Alternatively, get in touch with the National Childbirth Trust which has breast-feeding counsellors who are mums who have breast-fed themselves and know how difficult it can sometimes be. They will chat to you on the phone or visit you at home. For advice about your nearest NCT, telephone 01-992 8637.

BOTTLE-FEEDING

Advantages
1. Anyone can feed the baby.
2. You know exactly how much milk the baby has taken.
3. No embarrassment when feeding.

Disadvantages
1. You have to prepare the feeds and sterilize equipment.
2. There is cost involved unless you receive Family Credit.
3. Bottle milk does not contain antibodies to protect your baby against infection.
4. You have to carry bottles and equipment with you when you go out.
5. If the baby takes only part of a bottle, the rest of the milk must be thrown away.

Sterilizing the bottles

If you decide to bottle-feed your baby it's vitally important to sterilize all the feeding equipment. Warm milk is an ideal breeding area for germs, so everything must be carefully cleaned and prepared. You will soon get into a routine, however, and most mothers find it easier to make up a day's feed at a time.

Follow the instructions to make up the sterilization fluid or tablets. Fill the sterilizer with the fresh liquid. Teats should be cleaned first with washing-up liquid. Make sure there is no milk left inside the teat and clear the holes carefully. Clean the bottles with a bottle brush and rinse. All the feeding equipment should be put in the tank and completely covered in the solution so that there are no air bubbles trapped. Leave for the recommended time.

Steam sterilizers are a new method in this country, though they have been popular abroad for a long time. The initial outlay is high, but if you're thinking of having more than one child it's worth thinking about.

Boiling is an old-fashioned but effective method of sterilization and useful to know about just in case. All the feeding equipment should be completely immersed and boiled for at least ten minutes.

Never try to sterilize babies' feeding equipment in a microwave. Scientists have proved that it is almost impossible to sterilize items in this way.

Making up the feed

The feeds should be made up according to the manufacturer's instructions. Never be tempted to add an extra scoop of milk powder to a feed. This will increase the salt content to a too high level. Similarly, never add cereal to a feed unless instructed to by a doctor. This can cause choking and is dangerous. Once the day's feeds are made, store them in a fridge until needed. Babies will take feeds straight from the fridge but most mothers prefer to offer the milk at room temperature.

Safety first

Never warm babies' feeds in a microwave oven. The bottle will remain cool to touch though the milk inside may be boiling. The heat will also be unevenly distributed.

Points to remember

- To avoid the baby becoming 'windy', make sure the teat is far enough in the baby's mouth and that it is kept filled with milk throughout the feed.
- Watch the teat to make sure that the milk

flows evenly. Sometimes the teat collapses because the baby's strong suck causes a vacuum. If so, remove the bottle gently and start again.

- Babies should never be left alone to feed with a bottle propped against a pillow. There is a great danger of choking.
- Never save left over milk.
- Offer your baby boiled cooled water if he or she wakes well before a feed. Sometimes a baby is thirsty rather than hungry and will settle again without milk.
- Don't change your baby's milk without advice from your GP or health visitor. There is rarely any need to change the brand.
- Discard teats as soon as they appear roughened.
- If the teat seems to be be too slow for the baby, enlarge the hole by using a needle that has been first sterilized in a flame.
- Never carry milk for the baby in a thermos flask or insulated container. Milk should always be kept stored in the cool.

Use one of the specially modified cows' milks available. Never give a baby under six months old any other type of milk. Doorstep milk, evaporated or condensed milk, goats' milk and dried milk are not suitable. If you suspect that your baby has an allergy to the milk, speak to your GP *before* trying out the soya milks.

Whether you decide to breast- or bottle-feed, your baby will be fine. Make use of your local clinic to have the baby's weight checked as often as you wish. Your health visitor or GP will give you the extra reassurance you need, and you can compare notes with other mums.

For more information about feeding see Chapter 18; also crying Chapter 19 and sleeplessness Chapter 17.

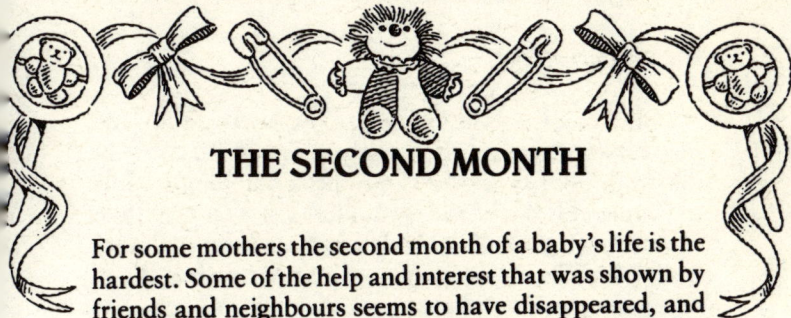

THE SECOND MONTH

For some mothers the second month of a baby's life is the hardest. Some of the help and interest that was shown by friends and neighbours seems to have disappeared, and the weeks of interrupted nights begin to take their toll and fatigue sets in. If this is how you are feeling, talk to your partner or friends. Perhaps the opportunity to have some extra rest or visit the hairdresser may be all you need to restore your spirits. Accept all offers of help – it's in everybody's interest.

At two months the baby is beginning to settle into a routine as you become more tuned in to its needs. It's amazing how quickly you know whether the cry is for food, discomfort or boredom. Of course there will be days when things don't go according to plan. These will usually be when you plan to go out shopping or visit a friend! Life's like that though, and tomorrow's another day. Try to take each day as it comes so that you don't feel resentful if the baby just won't go to sleep to fit in with your plans. Babies of this age can show signs of boredom and don't always want to be put to sleep immediately after a feed.

- Try carrying the baby in a sling around the house to leave your hands free for some light housework.
- Talk and sing to your baby as you move around.
- Use a baby bouncing chair so that your baby can see you as you prepare a meal.
- Above all, make time for a cuddle. Babies aren't tiny snuffly bundles for long. All too soon they become mobile and you'll be wondering why you wished they'd grow up!

Undoubtedly, some babies are easier to look after than others. Each has its own temperament and it may be that your baby is not the easiest person to handle. Talk to your health visitor about your feelings. Many mothers need time to grow to love their babies. Babies who are fretful, colicky or dissatisfied are harder to handle, so don't feel you're a failure.

It's about now that doubts sometimes creep in about your ability to satisfy your baby's hunger with breast milk. Don't give up unless you really feel that it is not for you. Offer more feeds at the breast for longer periods and your milk supply will increase.

Bottle-fed babies sometimes appear a little unsettled around this time, too. Don't be tempted to change the baby's milk – this seldom helps and can upset the baby further. Make up one more bottle than you think you will need and use this to top up the bottle if you feel your baby is still unsatisfied at the end of a normal feed.

Most babies gain about 28 g (1 oz) per day from about ten days until they are about three months with a spurt between three and six weeks. It is a regular weight gain that is important, so don't be worried if your baby only gains a little each week. As long as your baby continues to grow along the expected line of the growth chart, all is well.

Making comparisons between babies is of little use as the babies' birth weights will have been different and therefore their expected growth rate.

If you're worried about your baby's weight, talk to your health visitor.

DEVELOPMENTAL CHECK-UP

At six weeks your baby will have a developmental check-up with either the doctor or health visitor. It is the same check that the baby has when it leaves the hospital. In a way it's a safety check to ensure that nothing has been missed, so do make sure that your baby has it. Use the opportunity to talk about any concerns you may have about lumps, bumps or rashes. All babies have these and you won't seem over-anxious if you ask.

Your postnatal check will also be due at six weeks. In some areas this is done by your own GP; in others it is done at the hospital. This check is important to make sure that your body is returning to normal after pregnancy.

POSTNATAL CHECK LIST

The questionnaire has been compiled to help you get the care you need after the birth of your baby. It can be taken with you when you visit your doctor or used as a personal guide. Remember your life-style will change considerably after having a baby, so do give yourself time to adjust.

Everybody regains their figure at a different rate. Don't expect miracles. Pregnancy is nine months in duration and it can take nine months to get back to your former shape. Appropriate exercise can help.

Emotions
How are you feeling? ....
How have your children reacted to your new baby? .....

Rest
Are you getting enough rest?   YES   NO

Eating
Are you managing to eat proper
meals?   YES   NO

Feeding
Are you happy with the method
of feeding you have chosen for
your baby?   YES   NO

Your body
Are your breasts comfortable?   YES   NO

Have you got backache?	YES	NO
Have you had any further bleeding?	YES	NO
If you had an episiotomy you can expect tenderness and swelling from your stitches for about three weeks. Are you still experiencing pain?	YES	NO
Are you constipated?	YES	NO

(It can take some weeks for the bowel and bladder muscles to return to normal. You can help this process by remembering to practise your pelvic-floor exercises every time you go to the toilet.)

You and your partner

Have you made arrangements for your postnatal check and family planning appointment?	YES	NO
Some couples make love before their postnatal check. If you have, was it comfortable?	YES	NO

Help

Have you got anyone nearby who you can rely on for help?	YES	NO
Are you able to get out easily?	YES	NO
Would you like to be in touch with other mothers?	YES	NO

List compiled courtesy of Peaudouce.

What a postnatal examination includes
1. Blood pressure check.
2. Breast examination.
3. A check to ensure that the womb has returned to normal size.
4. Check upon any stitches.
5. Discussion about contraception.

The postnatal examination is an opportunity for you to mention anything associated with your recent pregnancy that concerns you. If you are not able to obtain all the information you require from your doctor, talk to your health visitor.

Finally, don't be fobbed off. If you think that something is not quite right or if you are still in pain, say so. If no one seems to take any notice, ask your health visitor for help. If she seems unsympathetic, go to your local family planning or well woman clinic. Remember that just as it takes nine months to have a baby it can take nine months to feel normal again. This doesn't mean that you have to put up with pain or discomfort. If you really feel that you are not getting the help you need, contact AIMS (see page 105). This organization will be sympathetic and will help you. Your health is vital to the well-being of your family, so don't be put off asking for help.

THE THIRD MONTH

Twelve weeks seems to be a magical date in some parents' minds. It is, then, that the terrible three-months colic is supposed to end. Hopefully, the baby has gained weight steadily from birth. Most babies at this age have a wakeful period during the day, when they like to be up and about and amused. That's OK so long as the baby hasn't decided to make the night the wakeful time (see Why Babies Cry Chapter 19).

At three months the baby usually likes to lie on its back with head central. When lying in the cot the baby will continually move its arms and legs. Hands will no longer be tightly clenched and the baby will be able to bring them into its line of vision.

When the baby is held sitting, its back will be straighter and its head will be held steadily for several seconds before dropping forwards.

When the baby is laid on its front it can do press-ups. When it is held standing it will bend and sag at the knees.

What can baby see?
At three months babies are delighted by faces, they turn their heads round to look at things and follow nearby movements of people.

When feeding time approaches the baby will anticipate the approaching breast or bottle.

When the baby is shown a toy within 15–20 cm (6–8 in) of its face it will follow it from side to side.

What can baby hear?
The baby will still be startled by sudden loud noises but will quieten to mother's voice. When you talk to the baby it will make sounds in reply. The baby will cry loudly when it is uncomfortable or hungry or annoyed.

When the baby hears its food being prepared, it will start to salivate and may lick the lips in anticipation.

If you are worried about your baby's hearing ask for advice at the clinic or visit your GP. One early clue to a hearing problem is when a baby is startled when parents appear by the cot.

What can baby do?

One of the most reassuring things that babies do at three months is to stare contentedly at the mother whilst feeding. This is one of the most pleasurable signs for mothers to feel that there is a real bond.

The baby will smile and coo as it hears sounds of preparation for feeding or bath time. Babies enjoy a playtime of singing, tickling and talking. At this age, most babies will hold a rattle or small toy for a few seconds, but will be unable to bring it into eye sight.

TOYS

Babies of this age love brightly-coloured things. Mobiles are useful, and can be hung over the cot, changing area or where the baby usually sits. Light rattles can be given, though they will be dropped almost immediately. Bright pictures or baby books can also be taped on to the cot sides or in the pram. Older children can be encouraged to make pictures or mobiles for the baby.

SLEEPING

By about three months, most babies sleep through the night. You may have one that doesn't. Babies vary a lot in their need for sleep and some are wakened easily by household noises. Some will be good for a week or so and then start waking again, perhaps because of a cold or other illness. Don't go to your baby immediately unless it is a real distress cry. Most babies wake briefly during the night. Sometimes a cosy sheepskin will help to reassure the baby and he or she will drop off to sleep again. Babies who fall asleep on the breast or bottle are often slow to go back to sleep on their own and may need further sucking. (See Sleep and Sleeplessness Chapter 17.)

If you feel the baby won't go to sleep unless it is fed, try offering boiled water or diluted fruit juice instead of milk. It does no harm to the baby to wake several times during the night, but it may well exhaust you. Ask for suggestions from your health visitor or friends.

FEEDING

Most three-month-old babies are content with their breast- or bottle-feeds. Boiled water or diluted fruit juice can also be offered if the baby wakes before the feed is due. Don't forget that too much drinking will stop the baby taking a proper feed and it will then be waking up earlier. If you think your baby needs something more to eat, discuss it with your health visitor.

Remember:
- Babies who are given solid food at too early an age cannot digest it properly and will have diarrhoea.
- If weaning starts too soon, babies may develop allergies because their gut is not ready to digest solid matter.
- Babies who are given solid foods too early have a tendency to become fat.

(See Feeding Your Baby Chapter 18.)

CLOTHING

By three months old most babies will have outgrown the first-size baby clothes. Make sure that socks and baby stretch suits are not too tight. Feet can be damaged by being cramped. Cut off the feet of stretch suits and buy larger-size socks or bootees to make them last longer. Choose clothes that are light but warm.

IMMUNIZATION

At three months the baby will be due for the first set of injections, although in some areas the first injection will be at six weeks for tuberculosis, but this is not common. You will be invited to the clinic or GP's surgery. Immunization is important because it lessens your baby's chance of catching potentially life-threatening diseases. It also lessens the chance of other people's

---

IMMUNIZATION TIMETABLE

At six weeks: (In *some* areas)	Tuberculosis	Injection
From three months:	Diphtheria Tetanus Whooping Cough	} Injection
	Polio	Drops by mouth
Five to six months:	Diphtheria Tetanus Whooping Cough	} Injection
	Polio	Drops by mouth
Nine to eleven months:	Diphtheria Tetanus Whooping Cough	} Injection
	Polio	Drops by mouth
Thirteen to fifteen months:	Measles Mumps Rubella	} Injection
School entry:	Booster dose for Diphtheria, Tetanus and Polio.	

children who are not able to be immunized being infected. Although diseases like diphtheria and polio are now rare, it is only because of immunization. If babies are not immunized these diseases will return.

Your baby will be offered protection against diphtheria, tetanus and whooping cough by injection, and polio by mouth. Side-effects, apart from a light temperature or redness where the needle went in, are rare. Despite all the TV and newspaper comment, whooping cough vaccine very rarely causes side-effects, but you will be advised not to have your baby immunized if your family has a history of epilepsy, convulsions or fits.

Talk to your doctor and health visitor about the immunizations. They will be happy to answer your questions.

'Can my baby have the injections without the whooping cough jab?'

Yes, but talk to your doctor or health visitor before making this decision.

'I didn't want my baby to have the whooping cough jab, but now I've changed my mind. Is it too late?'

Whooping cough vaccine can be given on its own, but it's best given as a triple vaccine. It's also best given during the first year, but it can be given later on.

'My baby seems feverish and the arm is red and slightly swollen. She had her injection today. Can I do anything?'

If she is feverish, it can help to give the baby some paracetamol syrup at bedtime. If a plaster has been put on the arm, take it off, some babies are allergic to plasters. If the feverishness persists call the doctor.

On the day

Feed the baby well before you go for the immunization (at least two hours if possible) particularly if your baby is prone to being sick.

Take along a favourite rattle, or dummy, and dress the baby in something easy to take on and off.

THE FOURTH MONTH

Four-month-old babies enjoy periods of kicking on the floor during the day. Take the nappy off, too, but protect the floor. Turn the baby on its tummy for a change and put some interesting colourful toys nearby. The baby may start to roll at this age, so never leave him or her alone on a bed or other raised surface. If you are going to use a playpen, now is the time.

Try to get out and about with your baby. Walks in the park or a rest in the garden near a bush with leaves will fascinate most babies. Don't be tempted to leave your baby too much alone, your presence is vital for security and happiness. Your baby is like a sponge soaking up everything around. If you don't allow enough time with you, talking, singing and playing, he or she will be less sociable and ultimately less confident. At this age, bath time is usually much enjoyed.

SAFETY FIRST

- Be careful not to leave small things, like buttons, coins or pins around, that your baby could swallow.
- Never leave the baby alone on a bed or a raised surface.
- Be careful of your cup of coffee. Your baby may make a grab for it and be scalded. Be similarly careful at meals.
- If you have been putting your baby to sleep in a basket, now is the time to buy a more substantial cot.
- Pets, although they may seem safe, may not like the sudden movements that your baby may make. Never leave pets and baby alone together.

SOLID FOOD

Feeding the four-month-old baby is a time of decision making. As a new mum you will probably be bewildered by the amount of baby food that is available. Which is best? When should you introduce a new variety? How much does baby need? What about drinks? The short answer is, it's up to you! You know your baby best. Start off with small quantities and don't be put off by what appears to be spitting out. Look on the food you give as tastes rather than meals. Your baby is still totally dependent on milk as the main source of food, so don't reduce this. (See Chapter 18 on feeding.)

Ask your health visitor for advice. She will be up to date on what is available and what is best for this stage. Home-cooked food can be given, but remember never add salt to baby's food. A baby's kidneys will not be able to get rid of salt and the baby may become ill. Sugar also needs to be given in very small amounts.

You will find that the contents of your baby's nappies will change, too, from the soft yellow motion of the breast-fed baby to a more orange-brown as a more varied diet is given. If the baby appears to get diarrhoea, then cut down on fruit.

The following is an idea of what a four-month-old baby may consume in twenty-four hours:

6 a.m.	Breast- or bottle-feed.
10 a.m.	Breast- or bottle-feed plus two teaspoons baby rice.
2 p.m.	Breast- or bottle-feed.
6 p.m.	Breast- or bottle-feed plus two teaspoons of puréed fruit or vegetable.
10 p.m.	Breast- or bottle-feed.

THE FIFTH MONTH

Five months is a good time for you to make a tour of your home to check that it is safe for your soon-to-be-mobile baby. Already your baby will be starting to roll and the cat's food, your handbag and plastic carriers will no longer be safe.

CHECKLIST FOR SAFETY

- Check all electrical appliances. Place all flexes out of reach.
- Buy socket covers for all electrical points not in use.
- Remove household chemicals from under sinks, by toilets, etc. Fit cupboard locks or place contents out of reach.
- Fit stair gates. These are also useful on doors to 'pen' the child in an area of safety whilst you do the cooking, etc.
- Check windows are safe, put on safety catches.
- Check any doors that are glazed and cover with safety film (available from good babycare stores).
- Fit cooker guards, fire guards, harnesses for high chairs and buggies.

It's not worth risking your baby's safety, so plan ahead, act now and prevent any accidents occurring.

At five months your baby will have become quite a personality. Although you are still the most important person in your baby's life, by now he or she will be able to amuse him or herself for short periods. The baby will learn most when you are there to anticipate needs, to retrieve a rolling ball or turn on the musical box yet again and, of course, to chat away. Some parents find it easier than others to get down on the floor and play, but it gets easier! Try not to regard your baby's playtime as a time to dash around and get everything done. The more you put in to playtimes, the more enjoyment you will share with your baby, because you will notice all the new things that he or she is suddenly able to do.

At about five months most babies love to use you as a trampoline, bouncing up and down on your lap with little sign of exhaustion. These sessions can be great fun, but don't take it as a sign that your baby should go into a baby-walker. Research has shown that baby-walkers can unbalance quite easily and can cause accidents. Also, the baby's spine is not yet strong enough to cope with long periods in a baby-walker or baby-bouncer. Don't be pushed into doing things just because a friend is, make your own mind up. It's your baby after all.

TEETHING

There is controversy about whether babies are upset by teething, but most mums notice that their baby is a bit more fractious than usual.

Dribbling is one of the first signs that teeth are on the way, then the lower gum will appear slightly red. Teething gel is available if you really think the baby needs it, but rusks or toys to bite on are just as good.

The actual age that the teeth appear doesn't matter. What does matter is that you start to brush your baby's teeth as soon as they arrive. Special small-headed baby toothbrushes can be bought. Clean the teeth twice daily using a fluoride toothpaste. Ask your dentist if fluoride drops would be helpful, too.

Try to cut right back on sugar in your baby's diet. Look at the labels on foods you buy. Many products have hidden sugars in them such as dextrose, maltose and fructose which are harmful to children's teeth.

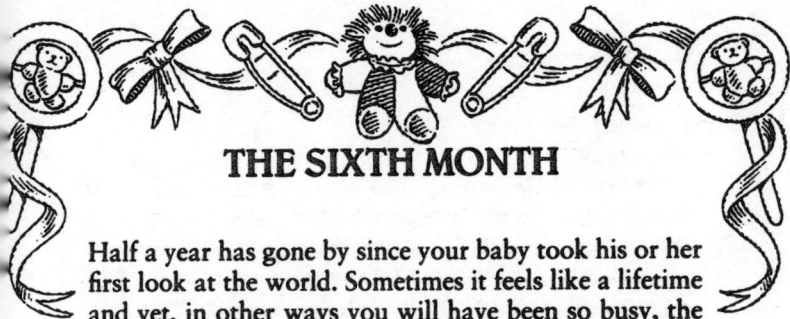

THE SIXTH MONTH

Half a year has gone by since your baby took his or her first look at the world. Sometimes it feels like a lifetime and yet, in other ways you will have been so busy, the days will have flown by. Six months is the time to take a look at things and make necessary changes. The baby will be much more amenable to change at this age, which is just as well as for many women this is the time when they will be returning to work (see Chapter 20).

THE BABY AT SIX MONTHS

- When the baby is lying in its cot it will be able to lift its head and look from side to side.
- If the baby is supported at the back and at the sides, it will be able to sit for short periods.
- When a friendly person comes near, the baby will raise its arms asking to be picked up. If baby's hands are held it will pull itself to a standing position.
- The six-month-old baby will kick and roll and bounce up and down when held in a standing position.
- Most babies at this stage are able to pick up toys with two hands. Most things will be taken to their mouth for further investigation. If the hands aren't being used for toys then the baby will be interested in its feet and will grab them.
- When the baby is being fed it will want to help hold the bottle or feeder-cup and will make little patting motions on the mother's breast.
- Babies of this age enjoy making sounds so try to provide different rattling or ringing toys. At six months babies will still be friendly to people they don't know, but will occasionally show some signs of shyness.

What can baby see?

At six months the baby is interested in everything around it. If there has been a squint it should have disappeared by now. If it hasn't ask your GP or health visitor for advice. The baby will want to get everything within its reach and will start to look for toys that it drops. The baby uses its whole hand to explore objects.

'What can baby hear?'

When mum or another familiar care-giver calls or talks to the baby it will turn immediately to that direction. The baby will chuckle and laugh when it is playing and shout with irritation when things go wrong. Other sounds the baby will be making are *mah, goo, ka* and it will react to the different sounds of the mother's voice.

Speech can be encouraged by giving baby the opportunity to talk to you, holding a pretend conversation. Try to speak slowly and clearly. Babies also start to enjoy books at this stage. Most libraries lend out board books and they will be delighted to encourage you. Babies that are read to will talk earlier, too. At this stage babies like familiarity so, when you look at the pictures, point out things that are part of your baby's world. A cuddle and book are a good way to start a bedtime routine (see Chapter 17).

TOYS

Six months of age is a wonderful time for exploring. At last your baby is able to sit, even though support is needed. Baby will lean forward and try to reach interesting objects, so make sure you have lots of colourful, light toys to shake and investigate. Activity centres are enjoyed from this age, too. Give your baby a couple of saucepan lids. He or she will love the noise!

Bathtime is also a lot of fun now as the baby kicks and splashes around. If you are not already using the big bath, now is the time to try. At first your baby may feel happier if you put the baby bath inside the big one, but, after a couple of days, most are happy to go in the bath. The mess will be a lot less, too! One useful piece of equipment that will save your aching back is a 'baby sitter'. This is a support which encircles the baby whilst it is sitting in the bath. Never be tempted to leave your baby alone in the bath – he or she can drown in a couple of inches of water.

FEEDING

Your baby will now be eating a variety of different tastes – fruit, vegetables and perhaps a little meat. At this stage you may begin to feel that your baby is ready for a bigger meal. This is best given around midday. Babies don't expect a pudding, so you don't have to give them one. If baby is still hungry, offer more vegetables. We all like to feel that we are giving the baby a treat however; so try to make the treat some stewed fruit or yoghurt. Gradually as the baby takes more at this feed cut down on the milk and, if bottle-feeding, offer the milk in a feeder cup. Breast-fed babies can be given diluted juice if you want to cut down on breast-feeding.

When you start weaning your baby from the breast, the midday feed may be the best feed to drop first. Your breasts will feel a bit overfull and uncomfortable at first. If so, express just enough milk to make you comfortable. Gradually the breasts will become accustomed to not providing a full feed at midday. Offer the baby a drink in a feeder cup away from the breast so that it doesn't smell your milk. Some mothers enjoy feeding their babies into toddlerhood, but this does not appeal to everyone. So make up your own mind. Your baby will have its own ideas, too, and may decide that enough is enough at six months or perhaps earlier.

Your baby will still need about 900 ml (1½ pints) of milk a day at this stage. The mixed feeding should still be seen as an extra to the milk, though it's a vital extra.

Vitamin drops, available from the clinic, should be given to your baby from six months of age until at least two years, preferably until five years. It is rare to find a baby with a vitamin deficiency. By giving the drops you are safeguarding your baby. Premature babies are particularly in need of vitamins.

At six months most babies are able to sit supported. You may feel that you want to buy a high chair to make feeding time easier. Don't forget to buy a harness at the same time. If you make putting it on a routine every time the baby goes in the chair, you will prevent the baby from having an accident later on. There are various types of high chairs. Some will fold up when not in use, some clip onto the table and some convert later to a table and chair. High chairs can sometimes be bought second-hand. If you buy one this way, make sure that it is still stable and that all the nuts and bolts are well tightened.

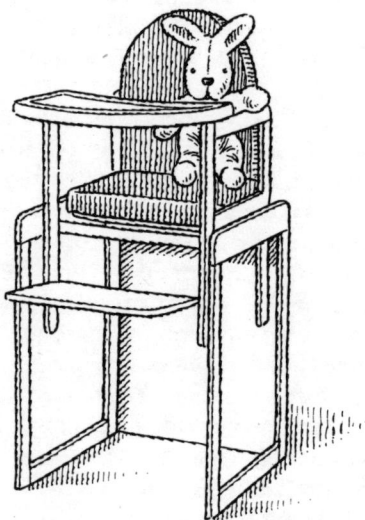

THE SEVENTH MONTH

For many babies seven months is the start of action. The baby is able to sit unsupported long enough to reach forward and grab a favourite toy. He or she will get into a crawling position, but will topple forwards or backwards after a few moments.

Try to vary the baby's playtimes by allowing longer in the bath, a period on a rug on the floor, some time with you in the kitchen, a walk to the shops. Babies get bored just as we do, so if in doubt go out. You only have to look out of the window around two-thirty every afternoon to see mums who have exhausted activities in the home, going out for a change of scenery!

Check in your local library or ask your health visitor where there is a mother-and-toddler club, or perhaps a one-o'clock club. These clubs will welcome you and you will be able to meet others in similar circumstances away from the confines of your home. Some mums enjoy getting together in each others homes once a week. Often these groups turn into mini playgroups which enable one mum to entertain two or three toddlers whilst their mums nip out to the shops or perhaps to the dentist.

Many local authorities run adult education classes where you can learn new skills or perhaps learn a language. If there is a need, many will provide a crèche, which would give you a chance to pursue something of interest, whilst your baby is well looked after. If your baby is particularly demanding, it really helps to have this sort of contact with others and it helps to have a purpose to your trips out.

Getting out and about with a small baby, can be difficult and it needs some planning particularly if you are breast-feeding. Luckily facilities are improving and many shops and public buildings are starting to provide changing and feeding areas for mothers and babies. Your health visitor will be able to tell you about local facilities. If there aren't any, perhaps a group of you can urge a local shop to provide a quiet room that's comfortable and clean. Look out for the National Infant Feeding and Changing symbol which indicates these facilities. There are many in the Mothercare and Boots stores.

If there doesn't seem to be much to do in your area, contact the National Childbirth Trust (see page 107). It runs postnatal groups and puts new mums in touch with one another. There's no need to feel cut off or lonely and if you feel shy about going to these clubs or groups try to meet one of the people that go first. Perhaps a chat on the phone will break the ice, at least you will know someone's name and be able to ask for her. Some areas have dads' groups too. There are more dads these days that share the caring, so it's natural that they want to meet up too! Ask in the library about local facilities and groups.

DEVELOPMENT CHECK-UPS

At seven months you and your baby will be invited to the clinic for a check-up. This will be done by the clinic doctor or health visitor. The baby's chest and heart will be examined, and the height and weight recorded and charted. Use the opportunity to talk about any concerns you may have about your baby. Remember that all babies develop at different rates and that some will be more active than others. Your baby may be better with its hands, whilst another may be well on the way to walking around the furniture. Don't get too worried if your baby seems a little slow, it probably means that it's better in another way – chat it over with your health visitor, she will be able to put you at ease or suggest help if necessary.

One of the most important parts of the seven-month assessment is the hearing check. You will be asked to sit with your baby on your lap, whilst one person distracts and the other makes different sounds behind your back. The baby should turn its head towards the sound. If the baby does not react, it may be because:

- The baby has been unwell recently, perhaps with an ear infection or cold.
- The clinic is too noisy.
- The baby is in a strange place and is feeling unsettled.
- The baby is too interested in everything else.

If your baby appears not to have reacted you will be asked if you have noticed any lack of response at home. Perhaps your baby may have been startled when you go to pick it up from the cot. Perhaps it doesn't turn when someone makes a noise across the room. These are all important factors and you are the best judge of whether or not it is a fair test.

If there is some concern about your baby's hearing, it will be checked again, often in a special clinic where the conditions are quiet. It's important that any problems with hearing are picked up early so that any necessary treatment can be started. This may be drops or perhaps further investigations by an ear, nose and throat specialist.

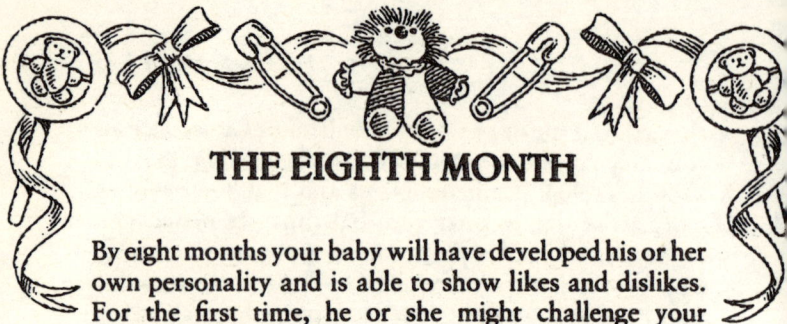

THE EIGHTH MONTH

By eight months your baby will have developed his or her own personality and is able to show likes and dislikes. For the first time, he or she might challenge your authority and try your patience. Having said that, most parents really enjoy being with their babies at this stage. Every day brings new advances and enjoyment. Perhaps your baby has discovered the 'drop-it-and-mummy-will-pick-it-up' game whilst sitting in the high chair. It is amazing how much they enjoy this, and it helps them to begin to understand that just because something can't be seen it doesn't mean it's gone for ever.

BABY-WALKERS AND BOUNCERS

Your baby will be wanting to be more active now and you may feel tempted to buy or borrow a baby-walker. You should remember, however, that these walkers are the cause of more accidents to young children than any other piece of equipment. It's all too easy for walkers to get a baby close to hazards such as fires or stairs, so think hard before you use one.

Baby-bouncers that hang from the door frame can be fun for babies of this age, but don't leave the baby in one for too long. Ten minutes is quite enough for a baby of this age. Most babies aren't meant to stand at this stage as their spine and leg muscles are not yet strong enough to support their weight for long periods.

OUT AND ABOUT

Trips out and about in the pram or pushchair will delight the baby, as will a trip to the swimming pool. Many pools these days have mother and baby swimming sessions when you can introduce your baby slowly to the water. Some babies hate it but others, often those who are fractious during the day, unwind and enjoy it. Do not allow your baby's head to go under the water. There is evidence to show that this is not safe for young babies.

If you are going to take your baby swimming more than two or three times a week, make sure that the baby does not swallow too much water. This is because the salt content is quite high in most pools these days. Don't keep the baby in the water for too long, however warm it may seem to you. Ten to twenty minutes is plenty. Dress your baby in close-fitting pants – accidents can and do happen! Take a towel to the edge of the pool so that you can wrap up your baby as soon as he or she gets out. Never take your baby swimming if it seems unwell or has a cold or ear infection. After swimming be ready with a drink and a rusk or a piece of fruit.

EVERYDAY CARE

Babies who are spending much of their time on the floor obviously get dirtier than cot-bound babies. It's helpful to keep a face-flannel with you in the kitchen to wash dirty hands, etc., during the day. Your baby will be a wriggler and you will have to make face-washing into a game.

Bathtime is great fun. You will still need to support the baby in the bath or use a 'baby sitter'. Once again, never leave your baby unattended in the bath. Babies of this age enjoy anything that floats, whether it's a sponge, an empty shampoo bottle, or a plastic duck. Take care not to let the baby grab the bath taps, which may be hot or possible to turn on. If it is likely to be a problem wrap the taps in face flannels.

Bathing with older brothers or sisters will also be enjoyable now. Just watch it doesn't get too excitable, especially if there are bubbles in the bath. Finally, get your protesting baby out for a nice rub dry. Most babies enjoy a firm rub at this age rather than the gentle patting of a few months back.

If your baby is still frightened of the bath, then continue to top-and-tail and do a bottom-wash in a small bowl. Let your baby play with the water in the bowl before you use it for washing.

Hair-washing can be a problem with some babies. If your baby is a screamer then try a shampoo hat, available from most baby departments. Many babies hate the shower spray, so if this is the case, use a plastic mug for rinsing instead. If your baby is still unhappy, wrap him or her in a towel while washing hair.

As your baby reaches eight months, you may find that the skin around the baby's bottom gets sore. This may be due to the baby sleeping through the night, without a change of nappy. It helps if you use a one-way nappy liner in terry nappies. This can also help with cheaper brands of disposable nappies. Nappy rolls can also be put inside disposable or terry nappies for extra absorbency. A good barrier cream, such as zinc and castor oil, will help to protect the skin.

During the day let your baby have a roll around with no nappy on. They love this, but be careful if they are bottom-shufflers as the carpet may burn them as they pull themselves along. Use a pair of towelling pants if this is the case and protect the floor with a plastic tablecloth covered with a blanket.

SAFETY FIRST
- Fit safety catches to cupboards.
- Alcohol can kill a baby.
- Full ashtrays can make a baby very sick.
- Keep toys free from stickiness or food as this can be a breeding ground for bacteria.
- Keep pets' feeding bowls out of the way.
- If your pet has an accident clean it up immediately using a good disinfectant.
- Don't let your baby come into too close contact with animals.

THE NINTH MONTH

Nine months is the stage when most babies become mobile. They may be crawlers, bottom-shufflers, backward-movers or swimmers across the floor. Some will have started to stand, bringing another area of the world into view. Nine-month-old babies are keen to try and try again so, to avoid frustration, it will help to remove any major obstacles to progress.

What can baby do?
- Sit alone unsupported for a few minutes.
- Crawl or move around the floor and pull up to a standing position.
- Walk with hands held for a few minutes and stand unsupported for a few seconds before sinking to the floor.
- Move from a lying to a sitting position.
- Show great interest in self-feeding. Hold and eat a biscuit, and possibly use a feeder-cup alone.
- Go rigid with annoyance when something goes wrong.
- Cling to familiar adult when faced with strangers.
- Play peep-bo.
- Put everything in his or her mouth, and show the object to an adult without being able to release it.

What can baby see?
- When sitting the baby will reach out for toys and examine them with interest.
- Everything will be grasped between finger and thumb, and baby will poke and point at things.

- Will look for toys that have fallen from the edge of a high chair or table and will enjoy hide-and-seek games.
- Will enjoy watching everyone around.

What can baby hear and say?
- The nine-month-old baby is interested in its own voice, shouting, listening to any reaction then shouting again.
- Will understand a few words: bye-bye, dada, mama, no, and babbles away tunefully to itself.
- May imitate adults' conversation or sounds such as coughing, etc.

TOYS FOR NINE MONTHS AND UPWARDS

There is a massive range of toys on the market aimed at this age group, which makes it very challenging to choose what is suitable. Read toy labelling carefully. If the label indicates that the toy is unsuitable for under one year then don't buy it. It will only bore your baby and gather dust. Try to pick a few things that will develop particular skills. Here are a few ideas:

- Two or three board books.
- Activity centre.
- Trolley with bricks.
- Soft ball with a bell inside.
- Stacking beakers.
- Pull-along toys.

Most of all your baby will enjoy playing with familiar everyday objects such as a plastic cup and spoon, saucepans and lids. Babies love music, too, so sing a few songs – don't be embarrassed, your baby will think it's wonderful however out of tune you are! Cassettes are useful too. There are hundreds available for children and many libraries will loan them out. Toy libraries are also a good source of toys. Look in your local telephone book or ask your health visitor if there is one in your area. It's also another good place to make friends.

FEEDING THE NINE-MONTH-OLD

Now that your baby is determined to try and help feed at meal times, finger-foods become even more important. Try little bits of cheese, soft pieces of fish or meat, boiled vegetables and pasta shapes. Little bits of fruit, provided they are skinned and have no pips, can also be given. You need to be sure that the pieces are small enough to eat easily, yet big enough to be picked up without being squashed to a pulp! Always stay with your baby while feeding is going on. It only takes a second for a baby to choke on a pea or piece of fruit. Because of this, crisps and nutty food should be avoided.

What to do if your baby chokes

1. Get the piece of food out using your finger if you can.
2. If the food can't be got out, turn the baby upside down and slap the back smartly until it is coughed out.
3. If you're still worried that it's not all out, call your GP or go to the casualty department.

By nine months, although the baby will still be drinking 900 ml (1½ pint) of baby milk or breast milk per day, most of its nourishment will be coming from solid food. Try to be as adventurous as possible and encourage your baby with food you have cooked for yourself (remembering to exclude salt and go easy on sugar). Try to eat at the same time as your baby – this really does encourage him. Don't try to force food on a baby, he knows when he's had enough. If you're not happy with the amount your baby is eating, write down what you offer at each feed for a couple of days and discuss it with your health visitor. As long as your baby is showing a steady weight gain all is well, but don't expect as much weight to be put on each week as in the first six months of life.

THE CLINGING BABY

All babies go through a clinging stage and it can be awfully hard, particularly if you are back at work. The baby who cries every time you put him down or go out of the room, or hangs onto your leg as you move around, can make life upsetting for the best of parents. Try to see it as a passing phase, because this is all it is. Meanwhile, adapt to doing things with baby on your hip, and try to take him with you as much as possible.

It does seem incredible that the younger baby is more trusting and ready to go to people than the nine-month-old plus. Auntie Flo or Grandma may have forgotten this stage, but it is a phase we all go through and it will pass. If you're off to work or leaving your baby while you go off shopping, say goodbye and leave quickly, having made sure you've got everything ready beforehand. Long drawn-out goodbyes only make matters worse, and the tears will probably stop by the time you are out of the street. Obviously babies will be less upset if they are left with someone they know, but now, during the clinging phase, is not a good time to go away for a weekend or overnight unless you have to. Talk to other mums; they'll remember how awful and distressing this time is. They will also remember that it is a passing phase.

THE TENTH MONTH

Hopefully by ten months your baby will be a companionable happy child, interested in its surroundings and moving around the furniture or pushing a brick trolley or other baby-walker.

Some may not be able to wait for the day to begin and will start waking early. Put a few toys in the cot, such as an activity centre, board books or a favourite rattle. A notice board which can be used to display bright pictures of animals or familiar things can also be of interest. Cassettes are invaluable and may soothe the baby off for a little more sleep. Creep in and turn the cassette on without letting the baby see you. Make sure it lasts at least half an hour!

There are some babies, of course, who won't be placated and who want food. Try offering water first because a regular milk drink at five a.m. will lead to regular waking. If that fails, try taking the baby to bed with you. It may work and if it doesn't at least you've tried everything! Sometimes shifting bedtime to a later time works, but you have to be persistent. Try half an hour or so later, but remember that it will take a few days of waking at the usual time before it works. Think about the baby's daytime sleep times, perhaps they could be better spaced.

WAKING IN THE NIGHT

This may happen after the baby has been ill and has enjoyed a cuddle or a drink during the night. Check there is nothing seriously wrong then, after a few words of comfort, leave. If the baby continues to cry go back again after a few minutes, offer reassurance and leave again. Try to leave it a little longer each time. By doing this your baby will know that you will come when really needed.

Your tiredness the next day will not be so easy to cope with. If it gets too much ask your partner to get up one night for you. If you can ask a neighbour or friend to look after the baby while you catch up on sleep. Don't feel embarrassed, we all need our sleep. (See Sleeplessness, Chapter 17.)

TIME FOR YOURSELF

Try to make some free time for yourself. It's very important that you feel happy and at peace with yourself, otherwise your relationships with your baby and partner will suffer. Try and get a baby-sitter so that you can get out one night a week, join a keep-fit or swimming class. Many of these have crèches. A few hours off during the day whilst your baby is at a friend's house can work wonders, particularly if you have a clinging baby. Try to arrange a regular time off with someone with a baby of the same age. It will be an arrangement which, with luck, will see you through to school time.

LOOK GOOD, FEEL GOOD

Don't forget to eat well. You can't feel good or look good if you don't have a balanced diet – and that doesn't mean a great deal of cooking which you may not have time for or enjoy doing. Buy plenty of fresh fruit and vegetables. Protein in the form of eggs, meat or cheese only needs to be eaten at one meal per day so you don't have to cook twice a day unless you want to. Do you need to lose a few pounds or tighten up some sagging muscles? If so, persuade a friend to come with you to the keep-fit class or tennis court – it's easier if there are two of you. Promise yourself a treat when you have achieved your goal.

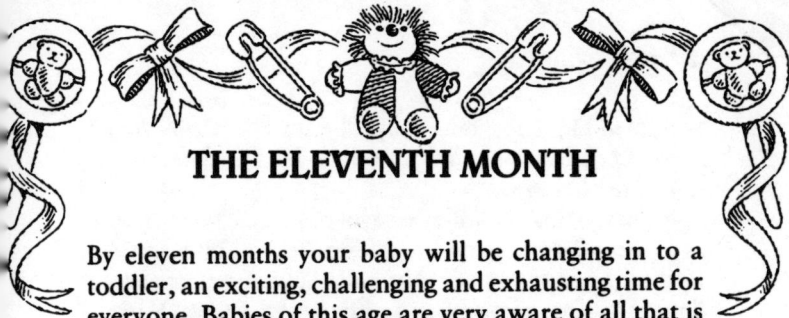

THE ELEVENTH MONTH

By eleven months your baby will be changing in to a toddler, an exciting, challenging and exhausting time for everyone. Babies of this age are very aware of all that is going on around them and want to be a part of it. Some are interested in other children and enjoy being with them; others need more time to become social beings.

At last life won't have to revolve completely around the baby's feeding and sleeping times. You will be able to amuse your baby if dinner is running a little late, and, if it suits you to keep them awake longer in the morning, you will be able to do this by going out shopping or to the park.

The bedtime routine is the only thing which should not be moved or changed if you have a settled baby. The routine of a meal, bath, story, cuddle, milk drink and into bed with a few songs, helps to soothe the baby slowly into an awareness that the day is coming to a close.

Around this age some babies seem to get 'night terrors' or wake crying for no apparent reason. A night-light in the room can help the child recognize the familiar surroundings and comfort itself. Others will need a cuddle. Don't offer a drink or it may become a habit. Never take the baby out of its room. This is fatal as they then resent being returned from the cosy atmosphere of mum and dad fussing over them.

One thing to watch is the time dad comes home. If dad's arrival coincides with the middle of the bedtime routine you will have problems. Babies of this age love a rough-and-tumble, but this of course excites them and makes them lively again.

Try to make bedtime a quiet period. A lot of night waking is caused by too much excitement just before bedtime. The baby falls asleep because it is physically exhausted, but wakes half an hour or so later because its mind is still active.

Babies of this age still need a lot of sleep. Twelve hours at night and up to two rests during the day. The daytime rests can become a battle of wills between mother and baby. How long you persist with these daytime sleeps is up to you. If you need a break during the day or if you feel your baby is over-excited, then put the baby in the cot with a few toys, and remain determined throughout the initial protestations.

WHEN TO SAY NO

Your newly mobile baby may want to explore every room and rearrange every cupboard, container or drawer. It will be up to you to decide the 'No-Go Areas', and refuse access to them by fitting cupboard locks, stair gates, etc. You may have to remove some treasured possessions until the baby is older. This is better than constantly having to say no. Babies of this age can be easily distracted, however, by the offer of a favourite toy or a drink. Do not use food as a bribe though.

There will be some occasions when you will have to say no. Baby will notice the change in your voice and your face. Try not to laugh when your baby is doing something you'd rather it didn't. If you do, the baby will receive a confused message of approval and disapproval. A baby covered in coal from the scuttle is a sight though, as are those who get their hands in the zinc and castor oil pot!

Do not expect too much from a baby of this age. Speak firmly, remove the baby from whatever it is doing and offer a distraction. In time, the baby will learn what is out of bounds. Some babies will react to the word 'no' by repeating what they have just done; others will burst into tears. All babies are different. Just persist in pointing out what is and what isn't acceptable.

TIMES OF STRESS

Keeping your temper during this challenging time is an art which is quite difficult for some of us, and which may need to be learnt. If you've had a busy day at work or if the baby has been ill and you've had a row with your partner, the last thing you will feel able to cope with is a difficult baby.

Talk to other mums about how they cope with stress and tension. There is also an organization which helps mums and dads in times of crises called OPUS – Organization for Parents Under Stress. (See page 107.)

CLOTHES FOR THE TODDLER

Toddlers' clothes need to be tough, easy-to-wash and easy-care. Tracksuits and dungarees are ideal, but make sure you buy sizes that allow for all the stretching and movement that babies do at this stage. Tight clothes irritate and restrict movements.

Check that the feet of babygros and socks are big enough for growing feet. Buy a pair of soft-soled booties (available from most major stores) and avoid buying real shoes until your baby is ready to run around outside. Shoes fitted before a baby is walking properly may not fit well once walking has started, so take your baby to a shoe shop that will measure your child's foot accurately. If you buy shoes that are too big your baby will be constantly falling over. Babies' feet should be measured every three months.

Winter clothes should be light and warm and preferably made of natural fibres, but these are often more expensive. Several thin layers are better than two thick. Babies hate being overheated. An all-in-one suit is a good idea for outside, so that there are no draughty gaps. Even if the suit has a hood, don't forget a hat. Mittens are also a good idea. To avoid losing them, cut a piece of tape about 60 cm (2 ft) long and sew each end to a mitten and thread through each arm of the child's coat.

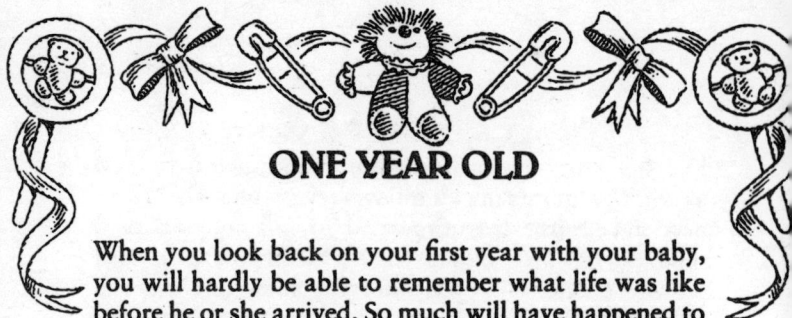

ONE YEAR OLD

When you look back on your first year with your baby, you will hardly be able to remember what life was like before he or she arrived. So much will have happened to you, your partner and above all to your baby. By one year most babies have trebled their birthweight and when you see newborn babies you will find it hard to believe that your baby was ever that size! Now, with so much personal experience to draw on, you can look forward to the fun of toddlerhood.

What can a one-year-old do?
- Sit well.
- Crawl and pull up to standing position holding on to furniture.
- Walk sideways around furniture.
- Possibly stand alone for a few moments.
- Walk with one or both hands held.

What can a one-year-old see?
- Tiny objects, like a piece of fluff on the carpet. The baby will delight in picking these up and examining them intensely. (Beware of things that can be swallowed or poked into ears or nose.)
- Things that are wanted, like toys, drinking cup or food. The baby will point to achieve his or her desire.
- Movements of people, animals, cars and so on. Everything will be watched intently.
- Familiar people will be recognized from some distance away.
- Hands, especially the baby's own! These will be examined minutely.

What can a one-year-old say, understand?
- Own name – recognizes and responds to it.
- Babble – talks continuously and imitates adults with great enthusiasm.
- Several words in context, that is mummy, daddy, walk, dinner time, dog.
- Simple order – give it to me, come to mummy, say goodbye.

How does a one-year-old play and behave?
- Drinks from a cup and holds a spoon.
- Less inclined to mouth objects and dribbles less.
- Enjoys making noises with toys.
- Puts things in and out of containers.
- Likes to be within sight of an adult, and will demonstrate love for people who are known.

By one year your child will be showing signs of co-operation, perhaps by helping when you are dressing and undressing him or her. Anticipation and excitement are expressed as you talk about lunch, going to the park or daddy coming home.

Great interest will be shown in anything you care to share with your baby, be it a leaf, a flavour or a picture in a book. Playtime is an important part of the day. It doesn't all have to be with you down on the floor, but it helps if you're prepared to help out when you hear a squawk of exasperation! Try to make time to play, look at books, sing and go for walks. This is a precious time and one that will soon be left behind.

By one year your baby is able to eat the same food as the rest of the family, excluding anything really spicy or fatty. Don't forget to omit salt from your baby's food and try to offer plenty of fresh fruit instead of sweet puddings. Your baby will be keen to feed and drink unaided.

INFECTIOUS DISEASES

As your baby starts to mix more with other children, the risk of childhood infectious diseases becomes greater. If you have taken advantage of immunization against diphtheria, tetanus, whooping cough and polio, these can be crossed off the list. If your child isn't protected already, it's not too late.

Measles, mumps and rubella (German Measles) can now be prevented by your child having the MMR injection at about fifteen months. Make sure that you take advantage of this immunization. It will save you many sleepless nights looking after an ill child, to say nothing of the side-effects of the illnesses themselves. The following is a guide to symptoms. If you suspect your baby has any of them consult your GP.

MEASLES

Incubation: eight to fourteen days from time of infection to outbreak of the illness.

Signs: runny nose, cough, reddened eyes, high temperature, nausea.

Diagnosis: 'Kopliks spots' appear which look like grains of salt on the inside of the mouth. Rash appears on day four or five, starting behind the ears and spreading in a blotchy way over the rest of the face and body.

Possible Complications
- Sore throat which may lead to an ear infection.
- Bronchitis and pneumonia.
- Conjunctivitis.
- Inflammation of the brain leading to encephalitis.

Care of the Child

- Bathe eyes as necessary using cooled boiled water. If the eyes are infected with conjunctivitis, consult your doctor.
- Keep temperature down by using paracetamol syrup.
- Offer plenty to drink.
- Call the doctor if earache starts, cough worsens, fever continues to rise, or if the illness does not seem to be getting any better.

MUMPS

Incubation: fourteen to twenty-eight days. At first the child may just seem off-colour, but then definite signs will appear.

Signs: Dry mouth, pain on swallowing acid things, swollen gland behind ear to under jawbone, face shape changes.

Mumps is not a very serious illness unless it is caught when adult, but there are some complications which it is wise to be aware of.

Possible Complications

- Deafness after infection.
- Check the infection has affected glands on both sides. If not the other side may be infected later.
- Very occasionally mumps meningitis can occur ten days later with high fever and a stiff neck. Call the doctor immediately.

Care of Child

- Offer lots of nourishing drinks through a straw.
- Help child to rinse out mouth.
- Give pain-relief if necessary.

RUBELLA (German Measles)

Incubation: fourteen to twenty-one days.

Signs: A rash of pink spots starts behind the ears and spreads to the forehead and rest of body. The rash may be so slight that you may hardly notice it. The glands high up on the back of the neck may become swollen.

This illness is not usually severe in children and needs no treatment. It can be disastrous for the unborn foetus during the first few weeks of pregnancy. If you suspect that your child has rubella, keep him away from women who may be pregnant and tell anyone you have been in contact with recently.

WHEN NOT TO HAVE A CHILD IMMUNIZED

Having seen all the complications that can occur if your child gets one of the childhood illnesses, you may wonder if there are any reasons why your child should *not* be immunized. However, immunization should not be done if:

1. The child has a temperature.
2. The child is being treated for cancer or leukaemia.
3. The child has an allergy to neomycin or kanamycin, or has had an allergic reaction to any other vaccine.
4. The child has had an immunization in the last three weeks.
5. The child has been given immunoglobin in the last three months.

The goal of the immunization campaign is to wipe out measles, mumps and rubella from the UK. This will only be achieved through immunization.

CHICKEN POX

Incubation: seventeen to twenty-one days.

Signs: At first the child may seem slightly off-colour, but suddenly red pimples appear that look like droplets of water. These turn to scabs and a new batch appears. This continues for three or four days. Usually the child does not feel too unwell.

Possible Complications

The spots may cover the body, including inside the mouth, ears, anus and vagina. This will cause terrible itching which will keep the child awake at night.

Care of Child
- It is best to get some ointment from the doctor for the itching. In severe cases a sedative may be given to help settle the child.
- The itching can be soothed by putting the child in a bath with a cupful of bicarbonate of soda.
- The spots will itch less if they are dabbed with a little calamine lotion which you can buy at the chemist.
- If you can leave the child's bottom uncovered for a while, this will help heal the spots.

SLEEP & SLEEPLESSNESS

Your new baby needs a warm, clean, draught-free room to sleep in. It is not necessary to buy a full-size cot straight away, though it will be vital later. Babies sleep just as well in prams, carrycots or cribs. It's a good idea to vary the location that the baby sleeps in, so that there will be no problems later when you visit friends or go on holiday. Perhaps you could use the pram for day-time sleeps and the cot for night.

Whether or not you let the baby sleep in the same room as you, is up to you. You may even choose to let the baby sleep in your own bed, but remember this can cause problems when the baby is more mobile. Any baby who has restricted movement, perhaps because of a dislocated hip plaster, should not be allowed to sleep in the parental bed because of the danger of suffocation.

Some parents find that they are easily woken by the baby's snufflings during the night, others find it reassuring and it makes the night-feed a little more bearable. Many parents start off with the baby in the same room with them, but move baby out later on. If you are unfortunate enough to have suffered a cot death, you may find that it is reassuring to have the baby in with you (see page 106).

Babies need a warm environment to sleep in, between 19–21°C (60–70°F) is ideal. If you feel anxious about the room temperature, ask your health visitor to check it for you. Overheating on the other hand can be dangerous, particularly for a very young baby. If the room seems comfortably warm to you then the baby should only need to be dressed in a babygro, cardigan and covered by two blankets. For safety and health reasons, don't use paraffin heaters in the baby's room.

How much sleep does a baby need?

All babies are different. Some seem quite happy on as little as twelve hours sleep per day, whereas others follow a pattern of feeding and sleeping throughout the day.

Things to consider when you want to put your baby down to sleep are:

When was baby last fed?

Was it a good feed? If so, perhaps you will be lucky and the baby may sleep for three to four hours. If it was only a small feed, anticipate that your baby may need feeding again in about an hour.

Is baby comfortable?

Remember the dangers of overheating and don't put too many clothes on the baby.

Some babies find sleeping on a sheepskin very reassuring.

Babies vary in how they like to be laid down. Some like to lie on their sides, others on their backs and some on their fronts. If your baby is inclined to be sick, make sure that you choose a side or front position, so that any vomit can dribble out easily.

Some babies like to be swaddled, that is wrapped securely in a shawl or blanket. Be careful that the baby's fingers can't get trapped in loose crochet work. In extreme cases this has been known to cut off the circulation.

What about changing nappies?

Some babies drop off to sleep at the end of their feed. In this case it's very tempting just to put them down to sleep without changing the nappy even if it's soiled. If you do this the baby may get a sore bottom. It's better to change the baby in the middle of the feed in order to avoid disruption at the end.

The drawback in allowing a baby to drop off to sleep whilst still feeding is that he or she does not learn to fall asleep in the cot or pram. This can lead to difficulties later when the baby may not be fed just before sleep.

Mobiles and music – are they helpful?

If started within two weeks after birth, some babies respond well to 'womb music'. These are tapes which play familiar sounds like the ones that baby would have heard in the womb. If the tapes are not started early enough the baby seems not to respond, perhaps because by then it is used to other household noises. Some mothers find that the tapes combined with a sheepskin help fretful babies to settle. (Addresses for where to buy them are given at the back of this book.)

Babies don't have to have total silence in order to sleep. Many prefer to sleep where they can hear the radio in the distance or the vacuuming. This is particularly so with second and subsequent babies, who have to get used to a high level of noise made by an active brother or sister. It's only sudden violent noises, such as a door slamming or an electric drill in the road, that are likely to rouse the sleeping baby.

Mobiles can also help a wakeful baby get to sleep. Musical mobiles can be bought, too, but enquire how long the music plays for. It's useless unless it runs for a good five minutes. Ordinary mobiles can be bought for as little as a couple of pounds. You can make your own using pictures backed with cardboard threaded on with cotton. It's often all that's needed to help the baby to doze off.

Routines at bedtime?

It helps the baby to anticipate bedtime if he knows that bathtime, a feed and a cuddle comes before going into the bedroom for a song or two, a look at the mobile and the pictures, and then into bed.

If dad comes home at bedtime the baby will naturally become very excited and worked up. It would be unnatural to try and avoid this happening, but it can cause problems.

My baby just won't sleep

Maybe your baby is one of those people who can manage on very little sleep. It's tiring for you, of course, and something that has to be experienced to be believed.

Write down how much sleep baby actually gets during the day. Keep the chart for a week and you may be able to see a pattern emerge of when the baby actually sleeps.

Some babies like being carried around in a sling while they are awake – this may have the desired effect of helping them to feel relaxed and sleepy too. For safety reasons, this is best avoided when you're cooking. A baby-bouncing chair is also wonderful.

If you have a big pram use it as much as possible. Most babies love them because they are so well sprung and bouncy. You can use them inside and outdoors.

Make the most of any offers of help and, if you can, put your feet up when the baby is asleep. Talk to your partner if you are feeling tired and see if between you a solution can be found. Talk to other mothers at the clinic and see what they have found helpful. Ask your health visitor for advice. She will have seen many mothers who have wakeful babies. Your GP may think it's worthwhile trying the baby with a sedative if, for instance, the sleep pattern has turned upside down with the baby asleep during the day and awake at night.

Above all, try not to let your baby's wakefulness and your lack of sleep get you down. At best, it is a phase that has to be got through. It's quite likely that when the baby is more active the sleep pattern will settle down. Some of us, however, just have to face up to the fact that we've got one of those babies who do not need sleep. If you feel under stress or desperate, ask for help.

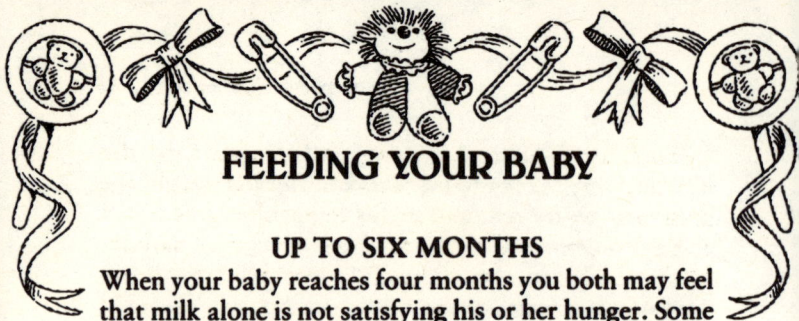

FEEDING YOUR BABY

UP TO SIX MONTHS

When your baby reaches four months you both may feel that milk alone is not satisfying his or her hunger. Some babies do become discontented at about three months, but usually an increase in milk feed is all that is needed.

First mouthfuls: Once you have decided that you are going to start weaning your baby, decide what time of day would be best. Preferably, choose a time when you are not too busy because feeding will take longer. A good baby-weaning food is baby rice. This is easily digested and, although bland in taste, it is accepted by most babies. Mix up the cereal according to the instructions, using water, modified baby milk or breast milk. Make up a little at a time. At first your baby may spit it out. If so, don't worry it's only the baby experimenting with the new taste and texture. Spoon it in gradually. Most mothers find this easiest to do when holding the baby on their lap, but baby-bouncing cradles are also ideal. (Never place the cradle on a table or raised surface. Hundreds of accidents are caused each year by babies bouncing the cradle off the table.)

If your baby seems reluctant, offer the breast or bottle first to help allay the initial hunger. If you have no success don't worry, leave it a day or so. If problems persist, ask your health visitor for advice.

After a week try your baby on a different taste. It's best to keep to savoury meals at this stage. Milk should still be the main source of food for the baby until about nine months, but the baby can be offered different textures. Mash or purée any fruit or vegetable until it is smooth. If you need to cook it first, don't add any salt, sugar or strong spices. Meat, fish, and cheese are best left until your baby is about six months old. Try one new food at a time. If your baby doesn't seem to like the new flavour, try it again a few days later. Food allergies are very uncommon. If you suspect that your baby is allergic to something, speak to your GP or health visitor.

Baby variety yoghurts can be given at four months, but leave adult varieties until six months because of the cows' milk content. Honey has been the cause of food poisoning in some babies, so do not give it to those under one year.

What can baby drink?

At this stage, milk is still the main drink of a baby but boiled water or fruit juice diluted half-and-half with boiled water, can also be given. There are many commercially prepared baby drinks. Make sure that they are well diluted as, despite manufacturers' claims, they often have a high sugar content. Never give your baby undiluted syrup in a dinky feeder. Even though your baby may not have teeth this can still cause serious damage.

ADVANTAGES OF COMMERCIAL BABY FOODS

- Easy to prepare in a hurry.
- Easy to mix up more when necessary.
- Useful when away from home.

DISADVANTAGES OF COMMERCIAL BABY FOODS

- Expensive.
- Ingredients not under your control.
- Taste and texture not like real food.

Many mothers use some commercial foods and some of their own home cooking. Just remember when preparing your own foods not to add sugar, salt or strong spices. Small amounts of food can be frozen in ice-cube trays and kept in a plastic bag in the freezer.

FROM SIX MONTHS ONWARDS

Once you and your baby are happy about solid feeding the quantity can be increased. At six months most babies will have a little baby rice at breakfast time and a small amount of savoury food at lunch time (or whenever the baby seems most hungry). (See month-by-month guide.)

Puréed meat and fish can be given mixed with vegetables. Remember that gravy or sauce should not contain salt. (Stock cubes, Marmite and Bovril are high in salt content.)

As the baby gets older and is able to sit up, finger-foods can be introduced. These are little pieces of food such as bread, cheese, peas or anything that can be cut up small. Never leave your baby alone when eating. Choking can happen on the smallest piece of soft food. Self-feeding does mean a lot of mess, of course, so protect the baby with a bib and put a cloth on the floor to protect the carpet!

What about lumps?

Once your baby is eating a wide variety of foods and is able to swallow successfully – usually about eight months – you can start to vary the textures of the food. Foods you have previously puréed can be mashed or finely chopped. As before, always stay with the baby during meals. Make the most of the time sitting down together by chatting and perhaps eating something yourself. Gradually your baby will want to hold a spoon. If you have one ready as well, it will help the baby not to become exasperated with hunger as the third mouthful drops off the spoon yet again! Feeding at this stage is messy. The baby will want to explore the food and will delight in making sticky patterns on the high chair. How much you tolerate of this is up to you!

The month-by-month feeding guide will give you an idea of the amount to feed your baby. You are the best judge of your baby's appetite and you will get to know when to encourage a little more and when the baby has had enough. Your health visitor will be happy to discuss any aspect of weaning with you. It's one of the things that worry first-time mothers most so, if in doubt, ask for some help.

What about drinks?

Usually babies of over six months have at least 900 ml (30 fl oz) of baby milk or breast-milk a day. Other drinks that can be offered are boiled, cooled water, diluted fruit juice and commercially-produced baby drinks. The amount a baby needs will vary dramatically from baby to baby. Just remember to offer a small drink when your baby wakes if it is not feed time. It is best not to introduce tea or coffee to a young baby. These contain caffeine, which is a stimulant, and is not helpful if you want a settled baby.

There are various feeder-beakers available when your baby is ready for a cup (usually around nine months, but earlier in some cases).

Try to make the break from bottles at this stage if possible. If the baby is only ever given juice from a cup then it won't be expected in a bottle. Babies who find it difficult to feed from a cup can be spoon-fed, but it's obviously a more time-consuming process.

Does a baby need sugar?

Sugar is found naturally in many foods such as fruit. In its natural form, it is not so harmful to the teeth and future health of your child. Manufactured foods, however, often contain high levels of sugar and it is often difficult to detect this on the label. Did you know that some sausages, baked beans and sauce mixes contain sugar? The 'no added sugar' flash on a pack doesn't necessarily mean the contents are not sweet. They may contain fructose, glucose or dextrose which are also sugar. 'Natural' may conceal the fact that the food has had spray-dried apple juice added or, in some cases, honey. It is hoped that manufacturers will soon realize that the public no longer wants this hidden sugar and will label their packages correctly in a way that can be easily understood. Sugar not only causes tooth decay and gum disease, but also obesity (overweight) which, in turn, can lead to heart disease, diabetes and strokes.

What about vitamin drops?

Vitamin drops are advised for all babies from six months to five years. They can be bought cheaply at the child health clinic. It is reassuring to know that your baby is receiving an adequate supply of vitamins in this easily acceptable form.

Modified baby milks

If you decide to stop breast-feeding for whatever reason, perhaps returning to work, you should change your baby onto a modified baby milk. Your health visitor will help you decide which one is most suitable. Babies should stay on baby milk until one year old, although pasteurized cows' milk can be given after six months.

Can babies be vegetarian?

Babies can be vegetarians provided they have a balanced diet, high in protein (beans, lentils and so on) and have 900 ml (1½ pint) of milk each day. The Vegetarian Society produces a very good leaflet (see page 108).

What about microwave ovens?

Microwave ovens are fine for cooking baby's meals, but *never* use them to warm the food or sterilize feeding equipment. In some cases, the food will heat unevenly (although the dishes will remain cool to the touch) and boiling hot food may be inadvertently given to the baby. Stirring well is not enough.

WHY BABY CRIES

There are many reasons why a baby may cry or be fretful, and you may feel that you have a baby who cries more than most! If this is the case, you will need all the help and sympathy you can get to see you through an exhausting time.

When a baby is fretful, the first cause a mother thinks of is feeding problems.

UNDERFEEDING

Babies who are not receiving enough milk will cry. If your baby is weighed regularly you will be able to see if he or she is getting enough food. If you are breast-feeding and your baby feeds less than six times in twenty-four hours, or is always sleepy and not feeding well, speak to your health visitor. If the baby has stopped gaining weight (babies usually gain between 170–225 g (6–8 oz) each week), discuss your feeding pattern with your GP or health visitor. A complete record of a baby's growth will need to be marked accurately on a percentile chart. A hungry baby is the easiest problem to deal with as more milk will solve the problem.

Remember, babies are individuals and will be more hungry at times than others. Be flexible and, when the baby needs it, offer more breast or bottle. The baby may well take less food at the next feed, but over the following twenty-four hours will probably take what you had estimated she needs.

If the hole in a teat is too small, a baby uses up all her energy in the first few moments and the urge to suck diminishes. The baby will then go to sleep only to wake crying with hunger a few hours later. Such a baby may appear to be difficult and demanding when simply enlarging the hole in the teat may solve the problem.

Some babies are sleepier than others, but gradually they wake up more regularly and stay awake for longer.

If you notice that the baby's nappies are not very wet this may be another symptom of underfeeding which will be corrected by a simple increase in milk. Your baby is the best guide for you to follow. If she wakes and cries and it is several hours since she was last fed, then a feed is probably what she needs. Don't try to make her last out until the estimated time of the next feed.

If your baby seems hungry even after a good breast-feed the problem may be that she is not taking enough of the nipple into her mouth when she sucks. Ask for help from your midwife or health visitor. Once the baby is correctly fixed on to the breast she will get enough milk and will stimulate the breast to produce sufficient for the next feed.

OVERFEEDING

Babies also cry if they are overfed. Just as we can experience discomfort if we lie down after a really large meal, so can a baby. Don't be tempted to add an extra scoop of powder to the milk mixture and don't ever add cereal or attempt to thicken a milk feed unless asked to do so by a doctor or health visitor.

It is very difficult to overfeed a breastfed baby. If you are bottle-feeding and think that you may be giving too much milk, try offering some boiled water.

When you think your baby is ready for solid food, ask your health visitor's advice. She will have guided many mothers and babies through the weaning stage. Most babies are ready for something extra at about four months or 5.5 kg (12 lb).

Remember:
1. Make up feeds accurately.
2. Offer boiled water if your baby seems thirsty.
3. Don't add sugar or thicken feeds.

WIND

Some babies seem more prone to wind than others and controversy continues between professionals about whether to wind or not to wind babies after feeding. A cuddle, with the baby held upright after a feed, may result in an expulsion of wind and this may be all that is needed. Other babies need a few minutes back-rubbing or patting before a satisfying burp is produced. Don't keep on rubbing and patting compulsively, some babies just don't need it. If your baby is inclined to 'possett' or sick up feed, wait until she has done her customary burp or possett before laying her down. Babies who are frequently sick after feeds will need feeding more often, but those who are violently sick after feeds should be seen immediately by a health visitor or doctor.

HELP WITH CRYING

Some babies cry more often than others. Some have a set time in the day when they are more restless and prone to crying. Constant crying is worrying and exhausting, particularly for the mother. Ask your health visitor for advice and see if there is a local support group, such as Cry-sis.

- Some babies respond to rocking or patting, singing or other kinds of music.
- Some hate being in a quiet room and settle better in a companionable environment.
- Many mothers find a baby sling invaluable.
- A brisk walk in the park or a ride in a car may also help.
- Sheepskins are extremely effective with some fretful babies, and womb-sounds played on a tape recorder have also had some success when started early enough.
- Many babies relax with a warm bath and massage, but others become even more fretful.
- Wrapping or swaddling may help.

COLIC

Crying can also be caused by colic, a severe spasmodic pain, which is very distressing for the baby. It usually occurs during the evening just when you are feeling most tired and have to prepare a meal for your partner. Most colic fortunately disappears when the baby is about twelve weeks old, but this is not much of a comfort to you or the baby, if baby is only two weeks old! Colic often causes the baby to draw up its legs in distress.

Warmth and rhythmic patting can sometimes help the baby, as can gentle pressure on the stomach. A hot water bottle can help if put in the cot and removed before baby is put into it.

- Try to have somebody supportive with you during this stressful time, so that you can share the comforting.
- If the crying becomes too much for you, put the baby in its cot and leave the room for a few minutes until you regain control. Let your tears come, it will relieve the tension.
- Get in touch with your local support group. There's nothing like another mum who's been going through it!
- Colic *will* eventually go away and, as you look at your calmly sleeping baby, you will wonder how you could have been so worried.

IS BABY ILL?

If your baby seems to be crying in a different way, it could be a sign of illness. If you are worried telephone your doctor, even if it is the middle of the night. You know better than anybody what is normal for your baby. If you cannot contact your doctor then take your baby to the nearest casualty department.

OVERHEATING

Babies need to be kept warm 19–21°C (60–70°F) by day and night. If you and the baby have been out, remember to unwrap the baby when you return. It can be dangerous for babies to become overheated. Also, babies that are kept too warm can be prone to heat rash and will also be thirsty.

In cold weather use a hot-water bottle to warm the baby's bed, but remove it before putting the baby in bed. Protect your baby from draughts by making a screen with a towel-airer or a cot bumper. It is best to dress the baby in several thin layers of clothing rather than one heavy outer garment.

In hot weather protect the baby's skin with a sun screen. A baby's skin is very vulnerable to sunlight and the baby will have many upset nights if she gets sunburn. Keep a hat on her head to protect her from strong sun, especially if you are using a baby sling. Babies are often more fretful in hot weather. If bottle-fed, offer them some boiled water; if breast-fed, feed more frequently.

NAPPY RASH

Nappy rash can cause a baby great discomfort, and some seem more prone to skin redness and soreness than others. If your baby has a persistent rash or soreness, ask your health visitor or GP for advice. To a large extent nappy rash can be prevented by thorough cleansing at every change. These days so many baby products are scented that it is difficult to find a baby wipe or lotion that does not cause more pain on an already sore skin. Cotton wool balls and water are often the answer. Use an unscented toilet soap for more thorough cleansing. If the baby screams when the area is touched, give her a 'bottom dip' in the bath. After drying baby's bottom, use a protective cream such as zinc and castor oil.

Prone to nappy rash?
- Use one-way nappy liners.
- Change nappies frequently.
- Cleanse baby's bottom thoroughly using unscented products.
- Allow baby to have some time with her bottom bare at each nappy change.
- If using terry nappies make sure they are properly laundered, preferably using a *non-*biological powder. Some fabric conditioners can also cause skin rashes.

There are many different creams available at the chemist which will treat nappy rash. Ask your health visitor or pharmacist for advice.

SKIN RASHES

Babies do have rashes and spots from time to time. Unless they seem to be causing the baby discomfort, it is best to leave them alone.

Heat rash

This is usually caused by overdressing or over wrapping and will go away when the problem is rectified.

Allergic rashes

These can occur if the baby has an extremely sensitive skin. Use unscented baby toilet products and wash clothes with a special baby soap powder. Make sure that the clothes are well rinsed and use fabric conditioner sparingly. Allergic babies are often more comfortable with cotton clothes next to their skin.

Infantile eczema

This is an allergy that usually runs in families. Either a parent or relative will have eczema or will be susceptible to hay fever or asthma. If you are concerned that your baby is developing eczema, consult your GP or health visitor. It usually starts on the face with red itchy patches on the cheeks and behind the ears. It is often found in the creases of the body such as the knees and genital area. Babies with eczema can be helped, so get advice as soon as possible. Your baby will be feeling miserable.

- Don't use soap and water – your doctor may suggest a mineral oil.
- Use cotton underwear.
- Make sure the baby's fingernails are kept short so that scratching will not cut the skin.

The doctor may suggest checking to see if the baby is allergic to cows' milk protein if you are bottle feeding. Soya milk can be tried, but this should only be done under a doctor or health visitor's supervision. Certain foods such as eggs or tomatoes may make eczema worse. Try to keep a note of the things that seem to exacerbate the condition and avoid them in the future.

The National Eczema Society produces a very informative newsletter and has groups in many areas. It can be contacted at Tavistock House North, Tavistock Square, London WC1H 9SR (01-388 4097).

Infectious diseases
(See page 74) Some can cause rashes, but babies, particularly those who are breast-fed, are very unlikely to get an infectious disease during the first six months of life. If you suspect that your baby has developed an infectious disease, take him to your GP or ask the GP to call. Remember to tell the receptionist if you think the baby may have been in contact with measles or whatever, so that you can be kept separate from other patients.

EAR INFECTIONS

Ear problems seem to be common these days. Occasionally they start as the baby begins to teethe, but they can also be associated with viral conditions or a high temperature. Babies become restless and fretful and cry out in their sleep. Often you will see them tugging or rubbing their ears, which shows that there is a problem.

In small babies an ear problem is not so obvious, so if you suspect that your baby is unwell, see your GP.

Ear infections normally respond to treatment with antibiotics, but pain-killers such as children's paracetamol are sometimes needed in the early stages.

It is important to get help quickly to avoid a burst ear drum and possible damage to the child's hearing.

If your baby has had frequent ear infections it is important to get the hearing checked at the clinic.

Very occasionally discharge, other than wax, can leak from the ear. This is usually caused by a burst ear drum. In this instance, the baby should be seen immediately by a doctor.

Dos and Don'ts

- Don't poke cottonwool buds inside your baby's ears. This can be dangerous.
- Don't apply heat to the ear as this can precipitate a boil or abscess to burst.
- If your baby seems unwell and off his food and you can't think why, take him to your doctor who will check his ears for you.
- If your baby has a high temperature, contact your GP immediately.
- When putting drops in a baby's ear, wash your hands, lay the baby on its side across your lap and, holding his head gently but firmly on one side, put in the correct number of drops. Try to keep the baby still for two minutes before you do the other ear.

EYE INFECTIONS

Many newborn babies have what is called sticky eye. This usually responds to being bathed with a salt solution. If your baby's eyes appear inflamed and sticky, then she may have conjunctivitis which is extremely infectious. The baby will feel and look miserable, and may well have a cold as well.

What to do for conjunctivitis

The baby needs to be seem by your doctor, so that drops or lotion can be prescribed. The drops can be put in the eye whilst the baby is on your lap. Wash your hands first, hold the eyelids apart and drop the solution into the inner corner of the eye. The baby will fight back whilst you are doing this, so it helps to have someone to put the drops in if you can't manage. As with ear drops, try to keep the baby still for a minute or two so that the solution spreads over the whole eye.

- It is very important to keep your baby's towels and flannel separate from others, so that the infection does not spread.
- Wash your hands before and after touching the eyes.
- If the eyes need bathing to remove the yellowish crusts, use a clean cottonwool ball for each wipe, and wipe gently from the inside of the eye outwards.

BEDTIME ROUTINE

The establishment of a bedtime routine will add to a baby's comfort. A baby gains security from the knowledge that, after a nursery rhyme and a cuddle and a look at a mobile, she will be tucked up in bed. The baby will soon recognize her teddy if teddy is always in the cot with her at bedtime even if away from home.

WHEN TO CALL FOR HELP

New babies can be the source of a great deal of worry to new parents. If you are anxious, ask for help from relatives, neighbours or friends. If they can't help, ask your midwife, health visitor or doctor – that's what they are there for. It can be difficult to decide whether a baby is ill or not, but trust your feelings.

You are the best judge of your baby's comfort or degree of discomfort. If you are worried about him – seek help. Don't be put off by receptionists who can't give you an appointment for two days. If you are worried about a baby under six months then a doctor or health visitor will see you. It's very hard to feel completely confident all the time about the care that you give your baby, and even a minor ailment such as a cough or cold can thoroughly undermine you.

If your baby has a cold

- Place a pillow under the foot of the mattress. This will help him to breathe more easily.
- Use a baby chest-rub to aid breathing.
- Give extra water or fruit juice.
- If the baby has a temperature, give children's paracetamol.
- A doctor should always see a baby with a bad cough – antibiotics may be needed.
- A vaporizer or steaming kettle may help the child to breathe.
- Cough mixtures are of little use to babies under six months.
- If a baby's breathing becomes noisy, difficult or painful, or if he sucks in his lower ribs and/or distends his nostrils, he may have serious respiratory trouble. Call a doctor immediately.

CROUP

This is a type of laryngitis which occurs in children because their respiratory tubes are so narrow. Whereas with an adult an infection in the larynx would give rise to a ticklish cough, with children it can cause sufficient swelling to block the larynx and cause a real emergency.

Croup can be recognized by a barking noise that the child makes after coughing. Breathing also becomes more difficult. Call a doctor immediately and make the room as steamy as possible (a bathroom is a good place). Stay in the room. After ten minutes or so, the baby will usually feel better, but wait for the doctor to arrive before coming out. In some cases it is necessary to admit the child to hospital.

CALL A DOCTOR IMMEDIATELY
- If you or your baby is ill.
- If your baby has a fit or turns blue, has quick difficult breathing, is hard to wake up, drowsy or unresponsive.

See your health visitor or doctor
- If baby becomes quiet, listless or floppy.
- If baby seems to have a temperature and refuses feeds.
- If baby has diarrhoea or vomiting, or both.
- If baby has a bad cough and noisy breathing, and can't breath easily through the nose.
- If baby cries in an unusual way, is not able to be comforted or appears in pain.

If baby seems no better after the doctor or health visitor has seen him, ask for more help – you will have no peace of mind while you are worried.

GOING BACK TO WORK?

If you decide to go back to work after you have had your baby, the first problem to solve is what type of childcare will be best for you and your baby.

Some parents are lucky and are able to share looking after the baby; others find that a grandparent, relative or friend is able to help.

If you have none of these forms of substitute care, then you will need to find another solution.

CHILDMINDERS

Childminders are women who look after babies and young children in their own home. They have to be registered with the local social services department, and have to meet certain safety requirements.

Your local social services can give you a list of local childminders and it's then up to you to decide, on the basis of visiting them, which one to choose. Anyone who uses their own home to look after children for more than two hours a day must be registered. If the childminder is not registered be wary.

Local authorities support children in a variety of different ways by setting up playgroups, training, and loaning toys and equipment. The childminder's home will be regularly checked to make sure it is safe and that she is not caring for too many children. Often the health visitor will also visit the childminders in her area. Childminders usually charge £35 per week or 90p per hour per child. The National Childminding Association will give further information (see page 107).

DAY NURSERIES

Most social service departments run day nurseries. Places, however, are very limited and are usually reserved for children with special needs. Your individual need will be assessed if you apply, but it's worth remembering that single parents or sole-earners will have priority over parents who are jointly earning more.

The day nurseries are mainly staffed by qualified nursery nurses and provide care from eight a.m. to six p.m. The average cost of a day nursery, run by the local authority, is assessed on ability to pay.

PRIVATE DAY NURSERIES

These may be run by private individuals or be part of a workplace nursery. The staff may not all be qualified, but the nursery will be required to have a certain number of staff to children. The charges for these nursery places varies from £30 to £60 per week depending on the area and facilities and are often considerably more for longer hours of care.

AU PAIRS, NANNIES, MOTHER'S HELPS

These are alternative forms of help which will mean that your child can be looked after in your own home. *Au pairs* are not meant to work for more than five hours per day. If you ask an *au pair* to look after your baby either restrict your working hours or pay more. Mother's helps are usually British girls who come to live with you and help out in a variety of different ways. Some have experience, but many do not, as with *au pairs*. The rate of pay for *au pairs*/mother's helps is £30 to £80 per week.

Nannies should be qualified and hold an NNEB certificate or similar childcare diploma. Those that are not qualified are really mother's helps. Nannies may live in or out and they charge £60–£100 per week depending on their experience.

RETURNING TO WORK CHECKLIST

Childcare

- Will it fit in with your hours of work?
- What happens if the baby or you are ill?
- Do you feel confident about the carer's ability? Do other children seem happy with her?
- Do you need to pay employer's National Insurance (check with local Department of Employment)?
- What about holidays?
- Think about agreeing a contract. A Nanny Contract is available from the Federation of Recruitment and Employment Services, 10 Belgrave Square, London SW1X 8PH. Please enclose a s.a.e. with request.

Yourself

- If you have a choice about when to return, are you feeling fit enough?
- If you are on maternity leave and feel unable to return at the given time, you will need a doctor's certificate.

The baby

- If you are breast-feeding, think about what you are going to do. Many mothers continue to breast-feed and either express milk for use during the day or bottle-feed and breast-feed before and after work.
- A few days before you return to work, have a practice run. It's surprising how long it takes to get organized in the morning. Pack the baby's bag the night before and make up any feeds.
- Introduce the baby to whoever you have chosen to provide day care. It will take time to feel confident that your baby is going to be happy while you are at work, but at least it won't all be new on the first morning back.

ON RETURNING TO WORK

At first you will probably feel very tired. Not only do you have to get yourself up and out, but there's the baby as well. Getting back into the work routine can be difficult too, and you are bound to have moments thinking 'I wonder if he's asleep now?' 'Has his cough got worse?' Of course, you'll feel guilty, most working mothers do. It helps if you have positive feelings about the nanny or childminder. She will be caring just as you would if you were there. Remember that in the early months a baby spends so much of its life sleeping that the process of getting to know the minder is fairly slow. Hopefully a close attachment will grow between you, so that you really feel that you are sharing the care.

Many women who have been anticipating returning to work find that when the day comes they just can't go through with it. Whatever you decide to do, it's not an easy choice. Talk to other working mothers and find out how they cope. There are Working Mums groups run by the NCT (Tel. 01-992 8637) and by the Working Mothers' Association (see page 108) which also publishes a useful booklet on returning to work.

Finally most babies do settle down and accept the separation from their mother, provided that the care they receive is loving and attentive. This won't stop you having occasional pangs, but remember the positive aspects of your absence. You have achieved a day's work, and you and baby are both delighted to see each other when you're reunited at the end of the day.

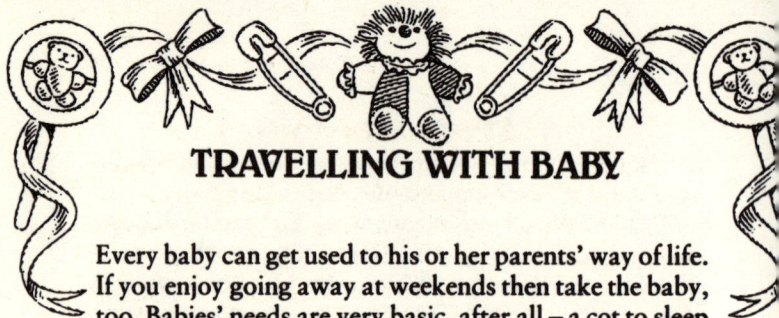

TRAVELLING WITH BABY

Every baby can get used to his or her parents' way of life. If you enjoy going away at weekends then take the baby, too. Babies' needs are very basic, after all – a cot to sleep in, food, changes in clothing and you! A lot of the paraphernalia that we surround ourselves with is unnecessary and certainly wasn't around when our parents had us. We can reap the benefits of disposable goods, ready-to-feed milks, and commercially-prepared baby foods when away for holidays or the weekend.

When you book, check what amenities are available. It really is a boon to have access to a washing machine and, if possible, a tumble-drier. Check if there is a kitchen with a fridge that you can use. This will make bottle and food preparations much easier – bottles can be made up as usual and stored in the fridge. If there is no kitchen, then take ready-to-feed liquid milk. There are no problems with breast-feeding.

BABY-SITTING SERVICES

Some hotels offer a baby-sitting service. This may be a 'listening-in' service by the telephonist which is free, or may be hotel or local people willing to sit in. In either case, make sure you are happy about leaving your baby and settle him yourself before going out. Leave a telephone number where you can be contacted in an emergency. Never leave your baby or young children unattended.

SINGLE PARENTS

If you are a single parent, contact Gingerbread (see page 106) which often organizes holidays for groups of single people who want a break. Consider taking a friend, relative or your parents with you.

GOING ABROAD?

If you are going abroad, make sure the baby is on your passport – this is something that can easily be overlooked. Your tour company should be able to advise you about the availability of baby foods and so on. To be on the safe side, pack an emergency bag of six nappies, wipes, four jars of baby food and a packet of baby milk. Make sure you have good medical insurance.

Before you leave, check that the baby or child's immunizations are up to date.

Items to take abroad
- Rehydration sachets (in case children have severe diarrhoea or vomiting – available on prescription or from a chemist.
- Paracetamol syrup or soluble tablets.
- High factor, water-resistant suncreams.
- Calamine lotion for insect bites or sunburn.
- Insect repellent.
- Suitable sucking sweets for take-off.
- Familiar favourite toys.
- Juice drinks with straw for the journey.
- Sunshade and sun hats.
- Cotton clothing and sheet for baby's buggy.

Some airlines offer skycots for transatlantic or long-haul flights. These need to be requested in advance. If you are going on a long journey (this applies to America) it is worth trying to change your baby's sleeping habits before you leave. Try getting him up half-an-hour later each day in the week before you depart, and put him to bed one hour later. Some GPs will prescribe a sedative for the journey.

Avoiding sunburn

Be careful about the sun. Not only is it dangerous for adults' skin to be overexposed without a sunscreen, it is also dangerous and painful for babies and children. Use a total sunblock or Factor 12 cream and keep your baby in the shade. The miseries of sunburn can occur all too quickly on babies' skin. Sunhats are also essential.

Diarrhoea and Vomiting

Both can be dangerous in a young baby. If either persists for more than a day, seek medical help. Restrict the baby to fluids only and, if the diarrhoea is severe, give an oral rehydration drink until it passes. Wash all fruit and salad well and, if the baby is over one year old, give bottled water to drink. Bottled water is seldom suitable for very young babies' milk feeds because of the high salt content. Ask the hotel if you can have boiled water from the kitchens.

Travelling with a baby or young children can be great fun, particularly abroad where, somehow, everyone is so welcoming to small children. Short journeys, once completed, will give you the confidence to go further afield. Talk to other families about where they have been, hotels that have been particularly welcoming, or good, well-equipped self-catering apartments.

SOURCES OF HELP

Association of Breastfeeding Mothers, 131 Mayo Road, London SE26 4HZ. Tel. 01-778 4769.

Association for the Improvement of Maternity Services, 21 Iver Lane, Iver, Bucks SL0 9LH. Tel. 0753 652781.

Association for Post-Natal Illness, Gowan Avenue, London SW6.

Association for Spina Bifida and Hydrocephalus, 22 Woburn Place, London WC1H 0EP.

Brook Advisory Centres. Address and phone numbers in your local directory under Brook, Family Planning Information.

Child Accident Prevention Trust, 28 Portland Place, London W1N 4DE. Tel. 01-636 2545.

Child Growth Foundation, 2 Mayfield Avenue, London W4 1PW. Information on normal growth rate of babies and young children particularly those with lack of growth hormone.

Child Poverty Action Group, 4th floor, 1-5 Bath Street, London EC1V 9PY. Tel. 01-253 3406.

Children's Legal Centre, 20 Compton Terrace, London N1 2UN.

Cleft Lip and Palate Association (CLAPA), Hospital for Sick Children, Great Ormond Street, London WC1. Tel. 01-405 9200 ext. 5289.

Community Health Councils. Address and phone number of your local Community Health Council in your local directory. Advice, where and how to get the service you need.

Compassionate Friends, 6 Denmark Street, Bristol BS1 5DO. Tel. 0272 292778.

Contact a Family with a Handicapped Child, 16 Strutton Ground, SW1P 2HP. Tel. 01-222 3969.

Cry-sis, BM Cry-sis, London WC1N 3XX. Tel. 01-404 5011.

Down's Syndrome Association, 12/13 Clapham Common, South Side, London SW4 7AA, Tel. 01-720 0008.

Family Planning Association, 27–35 Mortimer Street, London W1N 7RJ. Provides information on all aspects of family planning and methods of contraception.

Foundation for the Study of Infant Deaths, 15 Belgrave Street, London SW1X 8PS. Tel. 01-235 1721.

Gingerbread, 35 Wellington Street, London WC2E 7BN. Tel. 01-240 0935.

Haemophilia Society, 123 Westminster Bridge Road, London SE1 7HR. Tel. 01-928 2020.

Hyperactive Children's Support Group, 71 Whyke Lane, Chichester, West Sussex. Tel. 0903 725182.

La Leche League, BM 3434, London WC1N 3XX. Tel. 01-242 1278.

Marie Stopes House, 108 Whitfield Street, London W1T 6BE. For family planning advice.

The Maternity Alliance, 15 Britannia Street, London WC1X 9JP. Tel. 01-837 1265.

Meet-a-mum Association (MAMA), 3 Woodside Avenue, London SE25 5DW. Tel. 01-654 3137.

Mencap (The Royal Society for Mentally Handicapped Children and Adults), 123 Golden Lane, London EC1Y 0RT. Tel. 01-253 9433.

National Caesarean Support Association, 72 Perry Rise, London SE23 3QL.

National Childminding Association, 8 Masons Hill, Bromley, Kent BR2 9EY.

National Childbirth Trust, Alexandra House, Oldham Terrace, London W3 6NH. Tel. 01-992 8637. For sales (books, leaflets, bras, nighties, etc) Tel. 01-992 6762.

National Council for One Parent Families, 255 Kentish Town Road, London NW5 2LX.

National Deaf Children's Society, 45 Hereford Road, London W2 5AH. Tel. 01-229 9272-4.

National Eczema Society, Tavistock House North, Tavistock Square, London WC1H 9SR. Tel. 01-388 4097.

NSPCC, 67 Saffron Hill, London EC1N 8RS.

National Toy Libraries Association, 68 Churchway, London NW1 1LT. Tel. 01-387 9592.

NAWCH (The National Association for the Welfare of Children in Hospital), Argyle House, 29–31 Euston House, London NW1 2SD.

One-Parent Families, 225 Kentish Town Road, London NW5 2LX. Tel. 01-267 1361.

Parentline-Opus, 106 Godstone Road, Whyteleafe, Surrey CR3 0EB. Tel. 01-654 0469.

Parents Anonymous, 9 Manor Gardens, London N7 6LA.

Pre-School Playgroups Association, 61–63 Kings Cross Road, London WC1X 9LL. Tel. 01-833 0991.

Royal Society for Mentally Handicapped Children and Adults (See MENCAP).

Shelter, The National Campaign for the Homeless, 157 Waterloo Road, London SW1 8XF.

Sickle Cell Society, c/o Brent Community Health Council, 16 High Street, London NW10 4LX.

Spastics Society, 12 Park Crescent, London W1N 4EO. Tel. 01-636 5020.

Stillbirths and Neonatal Deaths Association (SANDS), Argyle House, 29–31 Euston Road, London NW1 2SD.

TAMBA, The Twins and Multiple Births Association, c/o 1 Victoria Place, Kings Park, Stirling KF8 3QX.

UK Thalassaemia Society, 107 Nightingale Lane, London N8 7QY. Tel. 01-348 0437.

The Vegetarian Society, Parkdale, Durham Road, Altringham, Cheshire WA14 4QG.

Winganna Natural Products, St. Ishmaels, Haverfordwest, Dyfed SA62 3DL. Tel. 06465 403.

Women's Aid Federation (England), 52–54 Featherstone Street, London EC1Y 8RT.

Working Mothers Association, 23 Webbs Road, London SW11 6RU. Tel. 01-228 3757.

FURTHER READING

Breastfeeding: Returning to Work (booklet) price 80p, plus 20p postage, from the National Childbirth Trust.

Money for Mothers and Babies (leaflet) free (send a stamped addressed envelope) from the Maternity Alliance.

The A-Z of Feeding in the First Year by Heather Welford (Unwin Hyman)

The Breastfeeding Book by Maire Messenger Davies (Century).

Entertaining and Educating your Pre-School Child by Robyn Gee and Sue Meredith (Usborne) £6.50.

Baby and Child by Penelope Leach (Penguin).

From Here to Maternity by Anne Oakley (Penguin).

You – After Childbirth by J. McKenna, M. Polden, M. Williams (Churchill Livingstone).

Birth–5 by Nancy Kohner (Health Education Authority) available from clinics.

Your health visitor may have free leaflets or videos to lend you, on the topics of babycare and feeding.

INDEX

THE FAMILY MATTERS SERIES

Anniversary Celebrations 0 7063 6636 0
Baby's First Year 0 7063 6778 2
Baby's Names and Star Signs 0 7063 6801 0
Baby's Names 0 7063 6542 9
Card Games 0 7063 6635 2
Card Games for One 0 7063 6747 2
Charades and Party Games 0 7063 6637 9
Children's Party Games 0 7063 6611 5
Dreams and Their Meanings 0 7063 6802 9
How to be the Best Man 0 7063 6748 0
Modern Etiquette 0 7063 6641 7
Travel Games 0 7063 6643 3
Wedding Etiquette 0 7063 6538 0
Wedding Speeches and Toasts 0 7063 6642 5

Forthcoming Titles
Card and Conjuring Tricks 0 7063 6811 8
Microwave Tips and Timings 0 7063 6812 6